Dear Farzaneh,

It was so wonderful meeting you and I look forward to seeing you again very soon.

I hope you enjoy this!

Warmest regards,

Gina

Sevenbennetts@verizon.net

Why "Going Soft" Will Make America Strong

GINA M. BENNETT
Counterterrorism Analyst for Twenty Years,
United States Intelligence Community

Wyatt-MacKenzie Publishing, Inc.
DEADWOOD, OREGON

National Security Mom:
Why "Going Soft" Will Make America Strong
by Gina M. Bennett

F I R S T   E D I T I O N

ISBN: 978-1-932279-72-6 Hardcover
ISBN: 978-1-932279-79-5 Paperback

Library of Congress Control Number 2008935783

Edited by Kim Pearson, www.primary-sources.com
Proofread by Bernie Panitch, www.verbatimediting.com
Index by Heather Hedden, www.Hedden-Information.com
Author photo by Vincent Lupo, www.directiononeinc.com

Wyatt-MacKenzie Publishing, Inc., Deadwood, OR
www.WyMacPublishing.com (541) 964-3314

Requests for permission or further information should be addressed to:
Wyatt-MacKenzie Publishing, 15115 Highway 36, Deadwood, Oregon 97430

Printed in the United States of America

Table of Contents

Part Three

Dedication

To the women of the United States Intelligence Community—a.k.a.—the most powerful, secretive, and intelligent sisterhood on earth.

FOREWORD

by Richard H. Kohn
Professor of History and Peace, War, and Defense
University of North Carolina at Chapel Hill
Former Chief of Air Force History, USAF, 1981-1991

IN THIS WISE AND ORIGINAL BOOK, THE DISTINGUISHED terrorism expert, Gina Bennett, combines her experience as a daughter, parent, and intelligence official to speak candidly about the chief national security threat we Americans face today. While she talks about the present and future, her views resonate powerfully with those of the people who founded the United States, and with the best who have been responsible for American national defense ever since. None were "moms" and their societies differed greatly from ours today. But they understood war, terrorism, and parenting from their own experience and from history. Were they alive today, they would be impressed by the sophistication, truthfulness, and profundity of Bennett's thinking.

When the members of the Constitutional Convention gathered in Philadelphia in the summer of 1787 to write a new frame of government for the infant United States, national defense was very much the first priority.

The framers of the Constitution had an expansive view of security, to include the cohesion of the political system and the loyalty of the population, as well as the economic health of the country. The United States was surrounded by hostile neighbors: Indian tribes to the west resisting American expansion; the British in Canada (and in forts they occupied on American soil) and in control of the Atlantic, shutting Americans out of their imperial economy; and Spain in possession of Florida and the area west of the Mississippi, indeed closing the mouth of the great river to American commerce. Worse, the states were more powerful than the central government, yet perhaps not able to keep internal order. Governor Edmund Randolph of Virginia, in presenting a new plan of union at the beginning of the proceedings, disparaged the old Confederation government: "Congress is unable to prevent war," "Not able to support war," and "Not able to prevent internal sedition or rebellion." Said another delegate, a "parental hand over the whole…and nothing else, can restrain the unruly conduct of the member states."

As a result, the Constitution created a government that could raise and support a military establishment, fund it, and use it to embark upon military operations in defense not only of the country but also of its interests abroad. The framers recognized that these, and other powers necessary for national security, could be abused. They empowered the president, as commander-in-chief, to control the military, but they feared executive power. From their reading of history and their own experience in two world wars (the French and Indian War in the 1750s and 1760s, and the War of Independence in the

1770s and 1780s were world wars), they recognized just how much war and foreign threats enlarged the power of the executive branch of government, and just how damagingly a state of perpetual war or indefinite danger (foreign or domestic) could erode the liberties of a free people. That is why they put the decision for war in Congress, the representatives of the people, and why they constructed a government of limited authority, shared and overlapping powers, and checks and balances. One of those checks speaks loudly to us today about the preservation of liberty: the Great Writ, as it is called, of habeas corpus, or the ability to challenge government when it imprisons someone without charging them with a crime and tries to hold them indefinitely. As the Constitution states, "The privilege of the writ of habeas corpus shall not be suspended, unless when in cases of rebellion or invasion the public safety may require it."

At the same time, by framing our national security policy and behavior in terms of child-rearing, Bennett's is a wholly original formulation. She questions whether "a terrorist group" really could "destroy our nation," and whether "we [are] failing to recognize other, more important aspects of our national strength." In terms that echo the founders of the United States, she writes that, "By expanding our definition of security to include our commitment to each other and our national character, we may find that our national security is not easily threatened. Our borders may once again be penetrated and our citizens attacked, but if we remain committed to who and what we are as a nation, and to seeing each other through any tragedy, America will always be strong and secure."

Her first advice is, as in child-rearing, not simply to react to the moment: "Our leaders should not allow America to be boxed into a reactive mode because of the actions of a handful of violent people" for "if we do, we are allowing the terrorists to diminish our freedom of choice."

She reminds us that like good parents, the United States must be consistent, act with calm, avoid overreacting, be fair, and set a good example by behaving in consonance with our policies and rhetoric.

She warns us about seeking absolute security at the cost of our freedoms and way of life: "Terrorism scares us personally, but it does not threaten our identity or shake our faith in democracy. If it did, then we should just hand bin Laden the keys to our country."

She points out that, like our children, our country not only needs to tell the truth, but the *whole* truth, lest it mislead or appear self-serving, and thus forfeit credibility. She reminds us that such is not easy either for children or politicians. But, as she puts it, "Only honesty earns us respect."

Bennett writes with the clear, cold eyes, the rigorous and precise analytical thinking, the deep experience, and the breadth of perspective of the best in our intelligence community—and as the successful mother of five children. This is a book every citizen should read, and every government official ponder, particularly judges, who in the end are responsible for preserving the integrity of the Constitution when the rest of the government gives in to fear, or the public's anger or panic.

She is very much in tune with the founding generation and with America's greatest war leaders when she concludes that while the threat of terrorism is real, and with weapons of mass destruction possibly catastrophic, terrorists can do nothing that the country cannot absorb. Compared to the threats of militarism, fascism, and communism arrayed against the United States during the 20th century by powerful nations and coalitions, terrorism is minor. It poses no danger to our independence or to our national existence unless we overreact, change our behavior or our policies, and voluntarily surrender our freedoms and liberties in the name of security. As a perceptive intelligence analyst and mother, Bennett writes that "No matter how much we spend on counterterrorism, no matter how aggressive, how successful, or how lucky we are in our efforts to prevent terrorism, there will be things we miss." In the end, "our national security is guaranteed by the strength of America's character, integrity, and trust in democracy." Thus "as long as we hold true to our democratic principles and have faith in each other, America will be secure no matter what challenges we face."

In this Bennett agrees with the founders of the United States. Five years after the Constitution went into effect in 1789, violence against taxes broke out in western Pennsylvania—the Whiskey Rebellion. President George Washington's advisers disagreed over the use of force. Alexander Hamilton wanted to send in troops immediately: "Government can never said to be established," he told the president, "until some signal display has manifested its power of military coercion." But Edmund Randolph, then the nation's first Attorney

General, argued for a more measured approach. "The strength of a government," he advised Washington, "is the affection of the people, and while that is maintained, every invader, every insurgent will...fear...its strength as if it were an unstoppable army." Or, as Gina Bennett puts it: "Each and every day we spend *without* thinking about terrorism, the terrorists lose.... As long as we persevere, the moms of America will render bin Laden and all terrorists like him irrelevant. And that will be their ultimate defeat."

PREFACE

from the author

I LEAD TWO LIVES. FOR YEARS I BELIEVED THAT MY LIFE AS a terrorism analyst in the United States Intelligence Community and my life as a mom were separate. But after twenty years of government service and fifteen years of parenting, I have realized they are not.

I have been in this "war on terror" for a long time. In 1993, I published a paper warning about Osama bin Laden and the extremist movement he represents. Ever since, most of what I have done at work has been a secret I could not share with my husband and five kids. But without their support, I would not be able to do all I've done. Over the years I have come to realize that everything I ever needed to know about national security, I learned from them. And all we need to do as a nation to ensure our security is to follow the advice we give our children. If only we had the courage to do it.

So often parenting is all about tough love. We teach our children the hard lessons of life so they are prepared to cope in the real world. This is how we pass on security—by helping them be independent and responsible. I can't help my daughter finish the science project she failed to start if I want her to learn accountability and responsibility, nor can I teach my son to be proud of who he is if I let him cave in to peer pressure. Teaching our children that life is not fair is hard. And it is also a difficult concept for us to face as Americans. No matter how much we spend on counterterrorism, there will be terrorists. Thousands of men and women will do all they can, but they are not going to be able to prevent all surprises.

We will survive if challenged again because our national security is more enduring than the absence of an attack. If we are on pins and needles, wondering every day if our government is going to be able to stop every plot, is that security? Isn't that the very definition of insecurity—constant fear and anxiety over what might happen?

The strength and security of my family is not dependent upon our home security system. It stems from the good example my husband and I set for our children and the unconditional love we consistently demonstrate. Our nation's security is not dependent upon the lack of terrorist attacks. Our security rests with the endurance of our values and principles of democracy and our commitment to them. Our strength is not the projection of power or the absence of challenge. It is the character our nation demonstrates *when* challenged that makes America strong and secure.

This book is not intended to be a rigorous, academic treatment of the origins of, or trends in, terrorism. I fully admit there are generalizations and simplifications of the complicated world we live in. This book is also not intended to be a commentary on previous administrations' national security and foreign policies. I do not believe foreign policy and security choices fall neatly into any political party's platform. It is merely the reflections of a mother who has been involved in counterterrorism for a long time. My hope is to encourage others to think about our nation's security in very different terms from the way it is typically depicted by de-mystifying the issue and describing it in terms that every parent can understand.

I have divided the book into *Three Parts*:

Part One describes how the rules parents try to live by also apply to making our nation strong and secure.

Part Two offers a discussion of how the lessons we teach our children are appropriate for our nation and imagines a day when our children are America's leaders.

Part Three takes some liberties with famous quotes about parenting to highlight the similarities between parenting and governing a nation. This section is meant to encourage parents, especially mothers who tend to be less inclined to engage in national security and foreign policy debates, to participate in important government decisions.

Part One

Redefining National Security: *A Parent's Perspective*

NATIONAL SECURITY MOM
MOM

PART ONE

Redefining National Security: *A Parent's Perspective*

PARENTS LIVE BY MANY RULES, INCLUDING THOSE WE TRY to follow to help us be better parents. Part One discusses how parenting truisms could just as easily apply to our national security.

While it is a gross generalization, many women probably would agree that they define security and strength differently from men. Ask a man what makes his family secure and he is likely to describe the dead bolts, security system, or barking dog, and possibly even the baseball bat or handgun he keeps hidden "just in case." He may think of his family's strength purely as an extension of its financial security.

Ask a woman. She may list some of the same things as part of the physical and material security of her home. But women also tend to see their family's security and strength as something esoteric. A family's strength comes from the love and respect family members show each other. Its security flows from the ability to retain that love and respect through the arguments, financial challenges, and emotional roller coaster of raising children. Both definitions are "right," but each requires a family to strive toward security and strength in different ways. A family is most secure when both visions are realized.

National security is not much different. It can be defined a lot of ways. There is no one "right" answer. But the definition that dominates today's discourse tends to refer to our physical security and safety from harm. During the Cold War we feared a Soviet first-strike, full-scale nuclear attack. Since the end of the Cold War, we endeavored to protect our borders from other types of military threats, such as missile and nuclear-proliferating countries labeled "rogue nations." Since the attacks on September 11, 2001, we have sought to protect our nation from terrorist attacks. Today, we often hear that terrorists threaten our national security.

Another way to look at national security, though, is to think of it like the extension of a family's security. A family is certainly threatened by a potential intruder. An arsonist may burn down a house. Family members may be hurt and certainly terrified. Would the family be destroyed, though, if they turn to each other for support and find the courage to rebuild their life?

Could a terrorist group really destroy our nation? Or are we failing to recognize other, more important, aspects of our national strength—those aspects that would in fact see us through another tragedy together? By expanding our definition of security to include our commitment to each other and our national character, we may find that our national security is not easily threatened. Our borders may once again be penetrated and our citizens attacked, but if we remain committed to who and what we are as a nation, and to seeing each other through any tragedy, America will always be strong and secure.

CHAPTER ONE

An ounce of prevention is worth a pound of cure

No matter how hard you try to prevent harm from coming to your kids, sometimes they get sick. Sometimes, they have their hearts broken. And sadly, there are times when they get seriously hurt. No matter how hard we try to keep Americans safe from harm, sometimes our preventative efforts will fail.

Chapter One

An ounce of prevention is worth a pound of cure

Every year when the weather turns cold, we go through the same battle in my family. I tell my kids to dress appropriately for the weather because "your body can only do one thing efficiently at a time—keep you warm or fight viruses." Despite my motherly wisdom, they go off in short-sleeve shirts without a jacket and hat. I always warn them that if they refuse my advice and then get sick, I will not be very sympathetic. One of my parenting rules is never make an idle threat, so when they do come down with the inevitable cold, I stick with tough love and let them suffer (at least a bit). I am hoping that one day, they will wake up and realize that I was right all these years and they will don their hat and coat without being asked. I am a mom. I have faith that day will come.

An ounce of prevention is common sense. Scientific proof aside, it makes sense for my kids to dress for the cold weather. It makes sense for us to lock our doors at night and turn on the back light of our house. It makes sense for a woman to be cautious walking in a dark, empty parking garage or on the streets at night. It is practical to use caution and prudence in reducing our risk of being harmed.

The same is true for our nation's safety in trying to prevent another terrorist attack in the United States. There is an important role for the preventative actions of our Intelligence Community[1], law enforcement, and Department of Homeland Security as long as we have reasonable expectations of their capability to succeed. America can't expect one hundred percent success in predicting every plot and preventing every surprise: no one has yet invented the crystal ball.

Our ability to uncover terrorist plotting against the United States will rest on a number of factors, including our success in keeping our intelligence activities a secret. That is particularly difficult for most Americans because we are a nation founded on the idea of transparency in government. Since the attacks on September 11, and the public airing of

1 The Intelligence Community is a federation of executive branch agencies and organizations that work separately and together to conduct intelligence activities necessary for the conduct of foreign relations and the protection of the national security of the United States.

shortcomings in the intelligence on Iraq's weapons of mass destruction capabilities, the public has had significantly less trust in the Intelligence Community. The need for keeping secrets may be as great as it has ever been right at a time when Americans want more oversight and scrutiny of the nation's intelligence activities.

I am not in a position to explain the entire effort on the part of the Intelligence Community to prevent terrorism any more than I can provide my children a scientific basis for why they should wear their coats on a cold day. But I can offer a little insight into the people who work every day to try to keep Americans safe. The Intelligence Community is people. They are just like everyone else in America. They hope to build a better future for their kids. They hope to pay all the bills this year and save for retirement and college funds. They want to make a contribution that matters. The only difference for those of us who work in the world of counterterrorism is that we also hope to save lives. And we hope to succeed without anyone ever knowing.

When my oldest son was five, his favorite superhero was Batman. One weekend I took him to work for a few hours so I could catch up on some paperwork. I did not think there was much he could infer about my work while sitting next to me in the middle of a typical government suite of nauseatingly neutral cubicles with no windows in sight. But I had forgotten that my boss had decorated our office space with wanted posters from significant terrorist events over the years. So my son did ask me why there was a picture of a man with a mask holding a gun to lady's head. Trying to recover from the idea that I might be scarring my kid for life by having him surrounded by all these images, I told him that they were just fake posters. But his curiosity was not completely satisfied, and he wanted to know what I was doing on the computer. I finally relented and explained to him that I was reading information on the computer and that I would send tips to policemen about where they could find bad guys. Impressed, he said, "Wow, you are like Batman. You work on a computer in a cave to help the police find bad guys." How true. Anyone who has ever worked in an underground vault of government cubicles knows a cave is a very accurate description.

Despite what you read in the novels or see in the movies, intelligence work and counterterrorism are not glamorous jobs. The vast majority of the day is spent literally slogging through data. It can be tedious, frustrating, and depressing. Amidst gruesome posters of terrorist attacks and within the dimly lit and sour-smelling, industrial-carpeted cubicle walls of hundreds of offices just like the one my son visited, my colleagues and I slog.

My son's visit to my office that day seemed inevitable. My first child, he was born in February 1993 three days before the first World Trade Center attack in New York. I date the birth of each of my children to a terrorist attack. It is sad, but my two lives are so intrinsically connected that a failure in one is as important as a blessing in the other. On that cold, snowy day in February 1993 when most of the residents of the Washington DC area were engaged in a milk-and-toilet-paper-buying frenzy, I was holding my first baby boy. When the phone rang in my hospital room the pain from my C-section was intense, but I did not want to miss the opportunity to share the news of my son's birth with a loved one. I reached for the phone only to hear my boss from work frantically saying, "Your people did this! Your people did this!" I had no idea what she was talking about, but about two hundred miles away in New York City where the snow was also gently falling, the unthinkable had just happened. On that morning of February 26, 1993, someone had bombed the World Trade Center. A terrorist had struck the very heart of New York, and although it would be years before it was generally understood, America was under attack.

My boss's frenetic phone call that morning was related to the work I had been doing in the fall of 1992 and early winter of 1993. I had been working as a terrorism analyst at the State Department's Bureau of Intelligence and Research. What led her to call me that morning was her belief that the World Trade Center attack was the work of a small collection of extremists we had been highlighting in our analytic work for months beforehand. My boss was right. Ramzi Yousef and his co-conspirators were exactly the kind of individuals we had seen popping up in Algeria, Tunisia, and Egypt. They were turning up in Tajikistan, the Philippines, Yemen, and even Burma; young men from over fifty countries whose backgrounds, families, economic status, and even religious practices were as diverse as they come. Yet they had one thing in common. They had all engaged in "jihad" in Afghanistan.[2] They all believed themselves to be "mujahidin" (holy warriors). In fact, sitting on my desk was an analytic paper I had planned to finish before going on maternity leave, "The Wandering Mujahidin: Armed and Dangerous." It described the connections between the breeding grounds for Islamic extremist groups that Afghanistan had become after the Soviet Union's withdrawal in 1989.

While my paper would have to wait until I returned from maternity leave, it was published in August 1993 and would serve as the first published strategic warning of what would later be called the "global jihadist movement" and of Osama bin Laden. In this analysis I warned that:

> US interests will increasingly become targets for violence from former jihadists because of a perception that US foreign policies are anti-Islamic; veterans of the Afghanistan jihad were becoming leaders of Islamic militant, insurgent, and terrorist groups around the world; the support networks and pipelines were flexible, decentralized, and generously funded, including by Osama bin Laden; bin

2 "Jihad" literally means struggle and is an important duty in Islam that is somewhat akin to the Christian sense of struggle against the temptation to sin. It also has a secondary meaning of "holy war," which traditionally is applied to a conflict involving Muslims defending themselves from aggressors. Since the Soviet Union invaded Afghanistan, brutally repressing its people, many Islamic scholars and leaders called the struggle a jihad.

This article would later be declassified and discussed by the media in August 2005, but in August 1996 when I wrote it, it was barely noticed. The Khobar Towers attack occurred and bin Laden's move to Afghanistan was not really a critical issue. Within a couple of weeks, I was back in the hospital having my second son. The summer of 1996 had proven challenging with bin Laden's move back to Afghanistan and the activities that led up to the Khobar bombing. At the same time, I had suffered from preterm labor with my second son and was on daily medication to prevent his early birth. I was very relieved when I reached full-term and he arrived healthy.

I had hoped to leave the government in 1996 when my second son was born, but within a few weeks of his birth, the small, nonprofit organization my husband worked for folded and he was out of a job. So back to work I went.

By early 1998, I had moved from the State Department to the Counterterrorist Center (CTC) of the Central Intelligence Agency. When I joined CTC in February 1998, I was pregnant with my third child. My first daughter was born a few weeks before the bombings of our two embassies in Tanzania and Kenya on August 7, 1998. While my role in helping would be extremely limited, I went into work with nursing baby in hand. Sleeping peacefully, she was exactly the sort of pick-me-up people dealing with the aftermath of such a disaster needed. My six-week-old daughter went to meetings that I never would have been able to attend. To this day, I still tease my former boss that he predisposed my daughter to keeping secrets from me. She has one of the best poker faces I've ever seen, even when caught red-handed snagging clothes from my closet to play dress-up.

In the fall of 1999, everyone had their eyes on the coming new millennium. While most of the US government was busy preparing for the predicted Y2K disaster, a tired and frustrated CTC was sorting through an ever-growing number of threats. Nonetheless, the millennium came and went with much fanfare, but no bombings. In what would be hailed as a shining success of foreign and domestic counterterrorism cooperation, the counterterrorism community identified and thwarted attacks planned by extremists for the millennium.

The 9/11 Commission report, in praising the Intelligence Community's "success" at the millennium, included a statement that struck me as very strange:

> Everyone knew not only of an abstract threat but of at least one terrorist who had been arrested in the United States. Terrorism had a face—that of Ahmed Ressam—and Americans from Vermont to southern California went on the watch for his like.

It would seem that the Commission believed Americans after the millennium were afraid of Middle Eastern-looking men because what they looked like could be an indication that they were terrorists. I hope that is not true. If it is, that would be exactly what bin Laden intended: for Americans to divide among themselves and be driven by fear to create enemies where there are none.

Unlike the 9/11 Commission, I do not recall Americans feeling the millennium period was a proud moment for their government's counterterrorism successes. In fact, it seemed to me that there was a stark contrast between the mind-set of Americans before and after the millennium. There is an unintended consequence to success. When I warn my children repeatedly that they will catch cold if they do not dress appropriately, the credibility of my warning depends on them actually catching a cold. Otherwise, if I warn over and over again and they never get sick, they conclude there is no reason to listen to me. Likewise, the credibility of the Intelligence Community's terrorism warnings start to diminish when there are no attacks.

When the potential Y2K disaster and al-Qa'ida-like attacks failed to occur, the two "exaggerations" were conflated into what resulted in an image of the US government having been "spooked." Many families canceled costly plans for millennium celebrations. For example, the mayor of Seattle, Washington, canceled celebrations at the Space Needle, out of fear of possible attacks. People are left not knowing exactly what to think when nothing happens. A popular columnist wrote an op-ed in the *New York Times* chastising the Intelligence Community for falling victim to bin Laden's "disinformation campaign." His accusation was exactly what many people thought: we had been duped.

The perception that the US Intelligence Community had exaggerated the threat posed by al-Qa'ida and had become obsessed with bin Laden had a lot to do with the skepticism with which the analysis was taken in the months prior to 9/11. Even the Cole bombing in October 2000 did not reduce the sense that the Intelligence Community was hyping the bin Laden threat. Instead, al-Qa'ida's choice of an American military target lent credence to the theory that bin Laden wanted to influence a broader Muslim audience by not conducting indiscriminate attacks and killing large numbers of civilians. It became difficult to persuade people to listen when they were beginning to think of us as "Chicken Little," always warning that the sky was about to fall.

What happened on September 11, 2001, is impossible to fully recount. It was a tragic day filled with extraordinary moments. On the other hand, I was doing something very typical that morning, vomiting with morning sickness. I was pregnant again in September 2001, though only a few people knew because I was still in my first trimester. Just a few days earlier, I had received approval to scale back my work hours. My father was in the last few months of struggling with severe complications due to his diabetes, and I was planning to spend more extended weekends with my parents. But the hours after September 11 turned into days and weeks, and it would be a long time before any of us knew what month it was.

After every terrorist attack, victims and their family members form important bonds to help each other through the tragedy. This was true from the Pan Am Flight 103 bombing in 1988, the Oklahoma City bombing in 1996, or even the Columbine High School massacre in 1999. After every attack, there are always efforts to investigate what went wrong and whether someone could have done something differently to prevent the tragedy. Unfortunately, the victims' family members and survivors are typically pitted against the community faulted for not being able to prevent it. The men and women of the Intelligence Community lost loved ones on September 11, just as we had in 1998, 1995, 1983, 1979, and almost every other terrorist attack against US interests. But there was no time after September 11 to mourn the dead. Colleagues, friends, and loved ones lost in the Pentagon attack or at the World Trade Center were only fleetingly remembered in a rare moment of silence when no one else could see the tear in your eye. There was just too much to be done to think about who and what we had lost.

The days and weeks that followed 9/11 went by without our realizing it. I can hardly recall seeing my family in those first few months, but I know I did. I must have seemed like a zombie to them. One December evening, I was trying hard to fall asleep. I realized after laying in bed for over an hour that I could not recall the last time I had felt my baby kick inside me. By this time I was over six months pregnant. I got up and drank a glass of juice and waited for some sign that the sugar had kicked in. Nothing. I finally called the maternity ward at the hospital where I had delivered all my children and spoke with a nurse. She told me to come in.

I kissed my husband and told him that I was going to the hospital to have the baby checked. He opened an eye, but what I said did not really register with him. The poor man had been both mother and father to our three kids for months. He was exhausted.

As it turned out, the baby was okay but I had been dehydrated and had had an infection that caused the amniotic fluid level to drop, leaving my baby sluggish. They pumped me full of liquid overnight and released me mid-morning. My colleagues were so alarmed that they brought me water bottles routinely throughout the day after that.

By the beginning of 2002, my baby was doing well, but my father was very ill. I will never forget my last conversation with my dad. He looked at me with a Santa Claus-like twinkle in his eye and asked how many more "pounds" until the baby was born, obviously confusing weight with time. I told him just two more "pounds" and his third grandson would be with us. He smiled and said, "Oh boy." Within a few minutes he drifted into a peaceful and seemingly painless sleep. I kissed him gently on his forehead—a place I had kissed him so many, many times. It had the usual light smell of my father's sweat and that salty dampness of his forehead. It may sound unpleasant, but this memory is of the last moment I ever touched or saw him alive.

On the morning of February 18, my sister called me to tell me he was gone. My father served twenty years in the Navy, spent another twenty as a defense contractor, and another seven as a civil servant for the Navy. When the two ensigns played "Taps" at his funeral, I finally cried. With one son on my lap and my daughter bundled up next to me, I allowed myself to show how weak I really felt. It moved me more than the mass or any other solemn rites of a funeral because Dad was the embodiment of service, not just to his family but to his country. And only after he was gone did I realize exactly how hard that service had been. I wish I had had the chance to thank him for it. I wish I had his strength. But more than anything, I wish I knew what his advice would have been with each new challenge I face in government service.

On March 4, my third son and fourth child was born, just a couple of "pounds" after I kissed my father good-bye. "They passed each other on the way," my brother said.

Years later, the 9/11 Commission would decide that the analysts in the Intelligence Community should have been able to "connect-the-dots" and figure out the 9/11 attack. The media would blame us, not just for failing to predict the attack, but also failing to prevent it. Connecting the dots sounds simple enough. Why couldn't we do it?

It is a lot easier to connect dots when you have the benefit of hindsight to tell you which dots to even bother connecting. In the weeks, months, and years before 9/11, we had so many individual dots that the pages were completely black. But even this description suggests that the so-called dots are something solid. Most information is as much a lie as it is a truth. Sorting out truth from lie is not quick or easy to do. Imagine trying to do an extremely intricate "connect-the-dots" game with barely visible, faded dots moving at varying speeds all over the page: that's a more accurate description of intelligence work.

Intelligence is not fact. Even an intercept of a conversation between the leader of a terrorist organization and a rank-and-file member is not a fact. They both engage in coded speak, using innuendo that only they can decipher because their language is immersed in cultural, religious, or personal histories. Above all, each is trying to manipulate or influence the other. If you think about your own conversations with a family member or good friend, you'll understand. Rarely do you exchange facts. You tell stories, refer to common experiences, empathize, and attempt to persuade each other. Or if you have ever tried following your teenager's instant-message exchanges, you know exactly what it's like to try to break into someone else's conversation and understand it. They are not exchanging facts.

No matter how much we spend on counterterrorism, no matter how aggressive, how successful, or how lucky we are in our efforts to prevent terrorism, there will be things we miss. An ounce of prevention is worth a pound of cure. But no matter how hard you try to prevent harm from coming to your kids, sometimes they get sick. Sometimes, they have their hearts broken. And sadly, there are times when they get seriously hurt. No matter how hard we try to keep Americans safe from harm, sometimes our preventative efforts will fail. But please believe me, the men and women who work every day in these efforts try as hard as they can and sacrifice more than can ever be publicly expressed. They do not do it for the money or the glory, that is for sure. They do it for their kids, for your kids, and for total strangers—because they believe we are all worth saving.

CHAPTER TWO

Time-outs do not solve everything

Like parents, our leaders should not allow America to be boxed into a reactive mode because of the actions of a handful of violent people. If we do, we are allowing the terrorists to diminish our freedom of choice.

Chapter Two

Time-outs do not solve everything

Time-outs are critical to the survival of both kids and parents. Only the invention of the baby wipe rivals the "time-out" as the favorite parenting tool in my house, where time-outs protect everyone and our dog from the flailing arms and legs of my toddler. A short time-out allows me or my husband to regain our cool and think more calmly.

But time-outs are just that: time out to assess the situation. Eventually you have to deal with what produced the incident. My toddler gets cranky and downright violent when she is hungry, overtired, or unable to communicate what she needs. The typical sibling rivalries and gender gaps irritate my twelve-year-old and ten-year-old. My high-school-aged son's desire for more privacy in a busy house is often at the heart of his rebelliousness. Everything turns into a debate.

When things get out of control in my house, a time-out gives me a moment to figure out who started "it" and why. Understanding the why—the root cause—of the incident is necessary if I am to have a prayer of figuring out how to prevent "it" from happening again.

Getting to the bottom of things is not a way to excuse bad behavior. It is a fundamental step toward resolving the actual problem with more permanency than a time-out. This is true for any kind of problem, from battles between siblings to confrontations between nations. When security experts discuss the need to identify root causes for extremist behavior, they are not being apologists for terrorists. They are trying to find out how "it"—the extremist ideology or behavior—got started, so they can come up with a more permanent way of preventing "it" from happening again. Just as parents must engage positively and patiently to reduce family tensions, our nation needs to engage constructively in addressing underlying problems.

There are many scholarly books that delve into the root causes of terrorism. There are terrorist groups motivated by an endless list of ideologies; not all terrorists today are followers of Osama bin Laden. While reading about the long history of terrorism is a worthwhile endeavor, it is not necessary for the purposes of comparing national security to parenting. It is enough to understand the common relationship between terrorists and the people and issues that they claim to champion. It is the relationship between the extreme fringe (the terrorists) and the ordinary people the terrorists say they represent that is often misunderstood. When we are unclear about how underlying issues relate to terrorism, we may miss potential opportunities to divorce root causes from the terrorists who exploit them.

Most terrorist groups are extremely small. It is not uncommon to see a terrorist group emerge from a larger, legitimate oppositionist or separatist movement that is trying to free itself of government control. These populations may feel politically, socially, economically, or religiously marginalized by their own government. The general population does not typically condone terrorism, but their intense frustration can lead them to stand aside and watch a handful of individuals communicate their angry message powerfully with the use of violence. Often, the population is caught in the crossfire between terrorist groups attempting to intimidate them and governments trying to repress them. When people are left with no realistic choice for their protection, they often keep as low a profile as possible. Outside observers will accuse some people stuck in such situations as turning a blind eye toward terrorism. It is easy to see how quickly entire populations can become painted as being associated with terrorists.

But the fact that a small group of terrorists exploit real grievances felt by a larger group of people should not be allowed to diminish the validity of the grievances. Suffering people end up watching in despair when their problems are discredited because the world associates them with terrorists.

Understanding the suffering of people is not being "soft" on terrorism, even if those people's grievances are being championed by terrorist groups. Understanding is a critical step toward figuring out how to diminish the influence of the terrorists.

With each of my kids, I can recall a temper tantrum thrown in a public place that seemed to be populated only by people who didn't have kids, who didn't like kids, and who were convinced they had never been kids themselves. All parents have experienced this: that embarrassing moment when you firmly believe that you are surrounded by people judging your parenting capability and your child's "normalcy." For a brief moment, you probably even think about grabbing your child and dragging them out of the store. Or you consider giving in "just this once" to your child's demand for chocolate cereal. But in your heart, you also know that you cannot let total strangers determine how you discipline your child.

Our policy choices about how to intervene in the world are not going to be easy, but we can start by understanding the complete picture. Like parents, our leaders should not allow America to be boxed into a reactive mode because of the actions of a handful of violent people. If we do, we are allowing the terrorists to diminish our freedom of choice. It is equivalent to "throwing the baby out with the bath water." If acknowledging root causes is dismissed as being "soft on terror" or excusing terrorism, then we lose our ability to decide for ourselves whose grievances are legitimate. And if we do so, we miss potential opportunities for breaking the cycle of violence. Given a nonviolent, viable alternative, people usually choose to reject violence. When they do, they deal the deadliest blow to the terrorists.

Chapter Three

Scrapbooking is a requirement

Turning a blind eye to another population's hostility toward America does not lessen the anger. It only guarantees the people will not listen to anything we have to say.

CHAPTER THREE

Scrapbooking is a requirement

WHEN I VISIT MY CHILDHOOD HOME, I OFTEN SHOW MY children photos and scrapbooks my parents kept of me and my siblings. My kids get so much amusement out of seeing me in my school uniform or my older brothers with their unbelievably long, hippie hair from the 1970s. As parents, we see it as a principal duty to retain the family chronicle. Mothers have often carried the load, especially with scrapbooks. But today's digital age has attracted more men to get involved. My husband enjoys creating digital photo albums and changes our photo slide-show screen saver with each season.

As parents, we can be obsessive in this quest to keep up our photo albums and scrapbooks. We want future generations to know who we were. We want our grandchildren and great-grandchildren to learn from us even long after we are gone. We are the family historians. We know that by being engaged in our children's lives, we are helping to shape their future, our nation's future. At the same time, we understand that if we do not embrace our past, we have no hope of creating a better future because we won't understand the foundation of the present.

The world we live in today is a product of its past just as my family is the result of the hard work and sacrifice of my parents, grandparents, and all my ancestors. Our past choices as a nation and our domestic and foreign policies have shaped our world. Recognizing this does not mean we are blaming past policymakers, condemning their choices, or challenging the rationale for them. It means we simply understand that they had a role in creating the world we live in today. And today's world is not a perfect place for everyone. By being the nation's historians, we can learn from missed opportunities, and yes, mistaken choices. We can do better each day, each year, and each decade by understanding the relationship between the past and the future.

Realizing our policy choices have ramifications long after the people who put them into action are gone is necessary for ensuring that our national security is not just a fleeting goal. We need to think beyond the next election and even the next generation.

Since the end of the Cold War and the advent of instant global communications, the world has become more transparent. The "have-nots" are far more knowledgeable about the "haves," and the disparity is not only wider, it is more widely known. Because the United States is the world's sole superpower, it is easy for much of the world to blame what is not going well for them on America. If they are poor, it is because we are rich. If they are powerless, it is because we hoard all the power, and so on. This is a backdrop of envy that America cannot really control.

Palestinians, Kashmiris, and Chechens, for example, have complained bitterly that America has abandoned its commitment to the self-determination of peoples by refusing to push Israel, India, and Russia, respectively, to recognize their right to independence. America's record of assistance to people in dire need in Darfur, Rwanda, and Bosnia-Herzegovina has been severely criticized. Even in places where America has intervened to create positive change, America has developed a reputation for quitting when the timing is right for us. The US support for Afghan "freedom fighters" warring with the former Soviet Union during its occupation of Afghanistan in the 1980s came to a near halt when Moscow withdrew its troops in 1989. The country was left in shambles with very little American aid to support its recovery. Many scholars have argued that America left the nation ripe for takeover by the Taliban, which later became Osama bin Laden's critical ally.

While we are taking our "time-out" to assess root causes

of terrorism, it is worth the discomfort to consider the extent to which past US foreign policies may be one of the root causes of the problems. Regardless of how well-intentioned we may be, there are many times when our activities do not produce the results we desired. There also are times when our intervention is perceived as hostile even when we hope to bring peace. As a nation, we cannot afford to delude ourselves into thinking that such hostility will go away. We have to understand the sources of it if we are to have any hope of changing peoples' minds. Too often, this kind of approach is seen as being "soft" toward our enemies.

As parents we do not think of ourselves as being "soft" on discipline simply because we try to see our child's point of view. If we are going to communicate effectively with our children and persuade them of something other than what they already believe, we have to understand why they believe what they believe, even if we think they are completely wrong to believe it. Any parent with teenagers will attest to how difficult this kind of communicating can quickly become.

My oldest son's transition to high school has presented a lot of new challenges in our household. My husband and I often feel at a complete loss for how to get through to him. It is hard for both of us to accept that it has been so long since we were teenagers that we are no longer familiar with the art of teenage speech or the challenges teens face. The one thing we have been able to do is identify the very moment our son starts to tune us out. We can see it in his face and body language. It is the moment he becomes convinced we do not understand nor are we interested in his point of view. So we have learned that every discussion we have with him has to start with listening—a lot of compassionate, patient listening.

Parenting a teenager can feel like navigating a difficult foreign relations crisis. You often feel you need a translator and a team of trained negotiators. Ignoring the communication challenge does not make it go away. Similarly, turning a blind eye to another population's hostility toward America does not lessen the anger. It only guarantees the people will not listen to anything we have to say. As we move forward, we have to keep our eye on the past and understand the ramifications of past US actions in the world. To communicate effectively with our allies, our potential allies, and even our enemies, we have to be sure we also listen.

CHAPTER FOUR

Actions speak louder than words

America has a unique

opportunity as the sole

superpower to lead by setting

a great example, and we

cannot afford to squander

it because America's time

as the leader may be as

fleeting as a parents' time

with their children.

CHAPTER FOUR

Actions speak louder than words

OF ALL THE PARENTING TRUISMS, THE HARDEST ONE FOR ME to follow is setting a good example through my own actions. I had great role models in my own parents, but it's been very difficult to live up to the standard they set. My mother never used a bad word to save her soul. My father was a sailor. I can hardly remember a sentence that didn't include a foul word, but he rarely lost his temper. They had different strengths, but together they offered a model of good behavior. I learned more from watching what they did than from listening to what they told me to do. Their actions were powerful. They showed their children to respect everyone, to think before acting, and above all, to be selfless.

I have a lot of trouble showing my kids how to behave. It's much easier to say "do as I say, not as I do." I have a tendency to take bold action without enough forethought. My philosophy leans more in the direction of "if you're going to do something half-assed, you may as well do it full-assed." These are not really behavioral traits I want to teach my children. I'm probably not alone. It is hard for parents to live each and every day as an example to children who are watching your every move.

But my kids are my kids. If not me, who else can I expect to set the example for them? From the moment they go off to preschool, the circle of people they began to emulate expands. By high school, a parent's example is hardly noticed. That does not give a parent much time to teach all the important lessons of life. This is why I berate myself every time I miss an opportunity to teach the right lesson by doing the right thing.

America has a unique opportunity as the sole superpower to lead by setting a great example, and we cannot afford to squander it because America's time as the leader may be as fleeting as parents' time with their children. While we have the opportunity, we should make the most of our leadership to demonstrate what we stand for. Our leadership has been viewed as hypocritical. Unfortunately, there have been times when we have been accused of saying one thing and doing another—something I can relate to as a mom.

There are several ways in which America is having difficulty setting a good example. Many people believe we have become so afraid of terrorism that we are willing to compromise our ideals of democracy to protect ourselves from attack. During the Cold War, America feared the threat of the Soviet Union. Yet, the United States was well-known for championing human rights, the self-determination of people, and the right of all people to live free from tyranny. I am no Cold War expert, but in hindsight it does seem as if America believed the best method for undermining Soviet influence was to illustrate the benefits of democracy. If drawn toward that example, nations would be more likely to reject communism.

To be a global power, we have to demonstrate that we are not obsessed with fear. Our influence must extend across the globe into Africa, Asia, South America, and beyond. Our example must be consistent, not just with what we say, but also in the way we interact with each nation.

Most people living in the nations of the Middle East want the same things that we do. Systematic polling over at least the past decade illustrates that the people in the Middle East want a voice in their governments. They desire multiparty politics, freedom of speech, press and congregation, free and fair elections, and an impartial judicial system. Yet, in some countries, the people are living under regimes trying to retain their hold on power at all costs. Look at Libya or even Egypt. Amnesty International has long documented Egypt's record of human rights abuses, noting in particular its concern that the "war on terror" is hindering human rights in

Egypt. Egypt's State of Emergency, in force since 1981, gives the government significant powers to use special courts, detain political prisoners, and limit speech. Political rallies result in crackdowns and arrests.

To the west in neighboring Libya, freedom of expression and association remain even more limited. Political oppositionists who live abroad complain routinely of harassment, and disappearances of political dissidents have not been resolved. There can be no mistake that these governments are in self-preservation mode. They are not interested in being accountable to their people or improving their lives. The people are often trapped between an authoritarian regime on one hand and Islamic extremists on the other, who try to hijack the entire opposition movement to achieve their narrow agenda.

The will of the people in many countries in the Middle East is a mysterious thing to be sure. Political Islamist organizations have appeal and can wield significant influence. It should not be a surprise. Muslims in the Middle East are almost all in agreement that Islam offers a model of justice, morality, and social welfare, even though there is tremendous debate about how to apply these principles to governance. The broad agreement can give Islamist parties, whether legal or not, the upper hand in opposing the corrupt and inept governments in the region. Very few of these political Islamist parties are extremist or proviolent, though. Most oppose various US policies, but they do not promote opposing the United States with violence or terrorism. The fact that they are critical of the United States is then exploited by regimes, like Egypt and Libya, to convince America that anti-US extremists would win if popular elections were allowed.

The history, culture, and societies in the Middle East are different. Given how our own nation was founded on mostly Christian ideals, I do not think we can determine that an Islamic form of democracy would not work. It would not be the same as ours, but if the people living under it believe it represents their needs, their hopes, their views, then who are we to judge?

When my children learn about early American history, I am always fascinated by what is *not* taught in our public schools. Naturally it is impossible to teach the whole story, so they have to offer the significantly abridged version. I am not complaining about what they learn, but I try to supplement it with some of the more complicated issues. Schools teach our children to be proud of their history, of their American heritage, and that is a great thing. In the process, though, they tell a story of men who seemed to inherently know the right course at every turn in the formative years of the United States. The "bad guys" were easy to identify. The "good guys" always did the right thing. But that's not what really happened, and I want my children to know that wisdom is hard earned. To be wise, you cannot just be lucky and get it right all the time. You have to deal with hard choices and make mistakes.

I teach my children that the Mayflower was not really an

intentional journey to start a free nation. It was an escape from religious persecution by some who ended up persecuting others. The Boston Tea Party had many negative consequences, including galvanizing support in England against the Colonists, and many of our founding fathers thought the saboteurs should pay for the destroyed tea. Even the Declaration of Independence was not talking about me or my daughters when it stated that “all men are created equal.” I am not trying to undermine what my kids are learning in school. I believe we live in a great nation with the best government the world has to offer. But I want my children to learn the truth, with all its complications and unpleasant realities, so my husband and I try to supplement their education.

One place we visit frequently to expand our children’s understanding of America’s early history is Colonial Williamsburg. The well-researched and highly interactive programs hold our children, as well as me, spellbound. During our visit we feel literally transported back in time as we live the events that were so important in determining the fate of our nation. My younger kids love dressing in costume and acting out events. More recently, though, my older boys have come to appreciate the subtleties of the history lessons. Colonial Williamsburg does a marvelous job in showing how difficult the decisions of each day leading up to and during the Revolutionary War really were. There are families whose loyalties are divided. There are characters whose choices were not clear-cut and who made tragic mistakes in spite of honorable intentions. Even Thomas Jefferson is forced into the very difficult position of having to explain how he could be an architect of the Declaration of Independence and yet own so many slaves. The realities of America's war for independence were complicated.

There were more confrontations than those that took place on the battlefield. The struggles included individuals and families trying to determine what was really in the best interest of their lives, the colonies' futures, and the extent to which the means justified the ends, no matter what the ends eventually were. The real battles of conscience and loyalty were far greater and complicated than a fourth-grade history book can convey.

The Middle East holds complicated and unpleasant realities too, as it struggles to determine its future. It can seem there are no realistic options for the United States in holding fast to its ideal of promoting democracy around the world while remaining constructively engaged in the Middle East. On the one hand, we cannot afford to lose our allies in the region abruptly. There are serious practical considerations, such as our need for oil. On the other, it would be risky to witness the rise of Islamist governments that would harbor hostility toward the United States. But can we abandon the promotion of democracy in this region without destroying our credibility as champion of democracy and freedom in the world?

Our actions should show the message we want to send—that America is the champion of freedom and places its faith in the will of the people. The peoples' choices likely will reflect both the region's Islamic heritage and the decades of anti-US sentiment that has been brewing. To accept the will of the people in the Middle East we may have to accept that we will not be popular. It would be natural to feel indignant about that; but no matter how hard we try, though, we cannot force people to believe in the same things we do.

As we push for democracy—real democracy, with free speech, free press, freedom of groups to congregate and organize—the results will be at times chaotic, disruptive, and uncertain. There will be ways of managing the risks inherent in this process through championing gradual reform and being crystal clear in our communication. The long-term result we hope for would be stability, predictability, and better governance in the region.

I hope that someday my children will look back and remember when I succeeded in setting a good example. I hope they appreciate how challenging some of those instances were (maybe once they are parents, too). I want my children to see that giving up doing what is easy and comfortable is worth the sacrifice, especially when your sacrifice can benefit so many others. If I set a good example through my actions, my children are far more likely to pay attention to my words of advice as well. As a nation, perhaps one day we may be able to enjoy the ability to influence nations by talking to them because we have a strong track record of positive engagement in the world and doing what we say we mean.

CHAPTER FIVE

A great cake is quickly consumed by nibbling at the edges.[3]

3 With apologies to Benjamin Franklin who really said, "a great empire, like a great cake, is most easily diminished at the edges."

Terrorism scares us personally, but it does not threaten our identity or shake our faith in democracy.

Chapter Five

A great cake is quickly consumed by nibbling at the edges.

There is nothing more decadent than a sinfully rich and moist chocolate layer cake. If only it contained no calories and no fat! I am also tempted by almost any kind of cookie. I am always appalled at my lack of self-control when it comes to a chocolate layer cake or cookies in our house. It is so easy to snag one cookie from the bag and think, "It's just one." But when you do that over and over throughout the day, you realize you have consumed half the bag! The cake is even worse. You take a tiny little sliver thinking that it won't completely kill your diet. But you justify just one more little sliver because the first was so small. Then another—it's a slippery slope.

The power of fear can lead to another kind of slippery slope. President Eisenhower once said, "If you want total security, go to prison...there you will be clothed, fed, given medical care, etc., the only thing lacking is freedom." No one wants to live in a prison, but everyone wants to feel secure. When you are made to feel insecure and afraid all the time, you are far more willing to accept your government's infringements on your rights. You want to be protected from…the enemy. And if the government cannot be precise about the identity of the enemy, then potentially the enemy is everywhere. And if the enemy is everywhere, the government must have ways of being on guard everywhere. Some governments do go that far, using pervasive and secretive security measures that invade privacy to monitor the activities of their citizens.

In April 2006, Osama bin Laden commented about America, "By allowing themselves to be fooled by lies and illusions, they will destroy themselves, ruin their countries, and lead their economies to bankruptcy." He believes we are playing right into his hands. With each infringement of our personal freedoms and every accusation that America is violating international law or abandoning its commitment to human rights, the terrorists must grin. I doubt bin Laden ever read President Eisenhower's quote, but he understands nonetheless that a nation will take extreme measures to secure itself. We have to ask ourselves whether the extreme measures would be worth the sacrifices. With all due respect to President Eisenhower and his quote, there are still murders and crime in prison.

An ounce of prevention does not mean forcing our children to live in a plastic bubble to prevent them from getting sick. Terrorism will be with us in some form forever. If we want total security, we could abandon health care and social security reform, the improvement of our public education, and our ability to rebuild after a natural disaster in favor of spending all of our national resources on security and the "war on terror."

Terrorism scares us personally, but it doesn't threaten our identity or shake our faith in democracy. If it did, then we should just hand bin Laden the keys to our country. Instead, we have to embrace that in order to preserve our democracy, we may be called to sacrifice a little security. Isn't that what the heroes of Flight 93 showed us? Like our founding fathers, they demonstrated that security is worth giving up in service of our country. Rather than hold onto those precious last moments of their lives, the passengers of Flight 93 sabotaged the terrorists' plan to destroy another government building. By giving up their lives to safeguard a symbol of US democracy, they demonstrated the way forward for all of us.

Like most Americans, I am tired of being afraid. I am worried about the increasingly heavier debt being left to my children so that we may feel "secure." Like many parents, I would like to see more attention spent on solving core challenges that face our nation: the economy, health care, education, and a whole range of localized issues that are fundamental to the lives of every family. Doing so does not mean we are abandoning our commitment to countering terrorism.

We can and should continually improve our intelligence, law enforcement, diplomatic, operational, and military capabilities to counter terrorism whenever and wherever it occurs. We will never be at an "end point." As the terrorists evolve, as the ideologies that motivate terrorism change, we will have to adjust and stay ahead of the curve. But even if we are successful and smart in the way we approach prevention, we will never be able to guarantee one hundred percent success. As a twenty-year veteran in counterterrorism, I would not want America depending entirely on the government's ability to identify every plot and prevent every incident. We will endeavor to do so and put our lives on the line, but like parents who risk everything to keep their kids safe, we may not succeed. There is a balance between allocating national resources toward prevention and spending money on those priorities that make our nation strong from within.

To preserve democracy, we have to give up the illusion of total security. The same is true of that chocolate cake. If I want to avoid the extra pounds, I have to sacrifice the satisfaction of eating it. And even if I only eat a little nibble here and there, the whole cake will be gone before I even realize what I've done. Democracy can be eroded completely if we convince ourselves that taking little slices of it is okay.

CHAPTER SIX

Life is not a fairy tale

I want my children to embrace life, to live their lives passionately, filled with joy and wonder. There will be many bumps and bruises along the way. And as they get older there will be heartbreaks and crushing disappointments.

CHAPTER SIX

Life is not a fairy tale

THERE IS NOTHING MORE HEARTBREAKING THAN WHEN our little girls discover they are not really princesses, or when our little boys give up on the dream of playing in the major leagues. But as parents, it is part of our job to prepare them for the fact that life is not a fairy tale, no matter how much we wish it could be for them.

This does not have to be the end of our children's dreams and aspirations. My little girl will be shocked when she learns that she is not going to find Prince Charming at the ball waiting to rescue her from her dreaded life with three brothers. I've always believed Cinderella would have been happy just achieving economic independence from her evil stepmother and stepsisters. What I hope to teach my daughters is that they will be happiest when they realize their own inner strength, when they are self-confident and know that they can pick themselves up after setbacks. Any woman who has survived an abusive relationship knows that to be able to stand on one's own feet is true security. No one can take that away from you.

I want my children to embrace life, to live their lives passionately, filled with joy and wonder. There will be many bumps and bruises along the way. And as they get older there will be heartbreaks and crushing disappointments. Cynicism and disillusionment will no doubt be part of their adult lives. But I would rather they experience life the way it truly is than live in isolation or lead a life of complete illusions.

The same is true for America. If we want to embrace our leadership in the world, it will not be easy. Engaging in the world can be as difficult for a nation as the first day of kindergarten is for an extremely shy child. There are so many people who may quickly decide they do not like you. Even when we try to be a positive force in the world, our actions may not be welcomed. America is often misunderstood. Sometimes we say the right thing in the wrong situation or the wrong thing in the right situation. It may leave us feeling as if it would be better to say and do nothing at all, just like my shy six-year-old who often quietly disappears into the woodwork to avoid being noticed.

I recently read a version of the classic *The Prince and*

the Pauper with my daughter and was struck by the idea that sometimes it would seem easier for America to just be "one of the regular guys." Instead, every move we make and every statement our leaders offer is scrutinized and criticized, like the prince in the story. If the world had no expectations of America, of our leadership, our foreign policy choices would seem so much easier.

But that is not really the future our founding fathers hoped to build for the new nation they fought so hard to forge. The authors of the Declaration of Independence purposefully wrote, "let facts be submitted to a candid world" because they sought the world's endorsement of the revolutionary process they were undertaking. They believed that the great new nation they were forming would be an extraordinary example of government. Having the approval of the rest of the world of their actions was important to their desire to influence a watching world.

Our founding fathers did not subject America to a perpetual popularity contest, but they did teach us that America's leadership has more influence when backed by the approval of fellow nations. Balancing the desire for this approval with an unwavering commitment to our principles is often challenging. There will be times when our choices and what we say will not be popular. Our soldiers and diplomats will be greeted with jeers and mobs rather than roses and smiles. The choices for our government's leaders will never be easy. They could be, if we withdraw from the world and lead a quiet, isolated, safe life. But is that what we want for our nation any more than what we want for our children?

Being a parent requires an unwavering commitment to teaching and loving our children no matter the challenges. We do not give up on them when they make mistakes. We do not give up on them when they turn their backs on us. We do not give up on our children, period. We tirelessly set as best an example as we can and always demonstrate compassion, flexibility, and unconditional love. America's leadership in the world will require the same compassion, flexibility, and unwavering commitment to our democratic principles even when the results may seem like anything but fairy-tale endings. Our kids may never truly achieve their childhood dreams, but the heartaches and fears that seemed so overwhelming in childhood will eventually fade. America may never have an easy day trying to be a beacon in the world for democracy and peace, but if we refuse to give up, people like Osama bin Laden would become as insignificant to our nation as the schoolyard bully eventually becomes to our kids.

PART TWO

What We Teach Our Kids Is Good Advice for America

NATIONAL SECURITY MOM
MOM

PART TWO

What We Teach Our Kids Is Good Advice for America

EVERY DAY WE PASS ON WORDS OF WISDOM TO OUR children. In the few short years they live under our roof we try to teach them all they need to know. We guide our children because we want them to succeed when someday they have to navigate this world without us.

My kids are lucky to attend a great elementary school, but it has a somewhat complex grading system. Every time the report cards come home, I marvel at how the teachers manage to monitor the progress of so many kids when they have to track so many different activities. Language Arts, for example, is broken down into oral communications, written communications, reading comprehension, and spelling. When I was in grade school, it was all just called "English."

A big part of my kids' report cards discusses "work habits." I was surprised the first time I saw how many aspects of "work habits" the teacher had to follow: accepts responsibility, complies with established rules, exhibits courteous behavior, exhibits self-control, follows through on assignments, listens to and follows directions, organizes materials, respects personal and school property, uses time constructively, and works and plays cooperatively. I look at this section of the report card and realize that the school is trying to encourage my children to be good citizens. I like that. I am glad their school sets these expectations and values them along with the fundamentals of language, math, and science. If my children learn these good work habits in school, they will be more likely to apply them in life as adults. And then they will be responsible citizens and good neighbors. Like all parents, I want my kids to succeed in life, to attend college, and to learn as much as possible. But it is far more important that they make a contribution to the betterment of humankind than to the betterment of their bank account. That goal begins with the good work habits expected of them at their school.

Someday I hope my kids will apply the lessons they are learning at school to their role as American citizens. I would like them to be active and passionate members of the electorate. I dream of their being engaged in their own governance. My kids may think I'm a little quirky when I go around singing the preamble to the

Constitution (still the only way I can recite it thanks to *Schoolhouse Rock!*), but they understand that I am just trying to inspire them. I never stop telling them how lucky they are to live in this country. I also never spare them the hard details of life for children in other parts of the world. I want them to know how fortunate they are, but above all I want them to value their good fortune and never squander it.

I believe that my kids, like so many others, could be great leaders of our nation someday. If they follow the advice of their parents and live up to the expectations set by their schools, they will be. The advice we give our children every day is exactly the advice we would wish our leaders to follow as they govern us and demonstrate America's leadership in the world. Because what we teach our children is what we should do collectively as a nation.

CHAPTER SEVEN

Tell the truth

Understanding the reality of the world we live in does not make our choices any easier. When our children are leading America, perhaps the best we can hope for is that they will be humble enough to admit that the truth is unclear.

CHAPTER SEVEN

Tell the truth

ONE DAY MY TWELVE-YEAR-OLD SON WILL HAVE A girlfriend, and when that day comes, he might voluntarily brush his teeth every day, maybe even more than once. Until then, we'll go through the same routine. He won't brush his teeth unless I tell him to do so. Believe it or not, one time I asked him, "Did you brush your teeth," suspecting that he had not. He said, "Yeah, I did." I was suspicious. I then said, "I mean today." He responded, "Oh, no. I thought you just meant have I ever brushed my teeth." The original answer was not a lie per se, but nor was it the whole truth.

I suppose in a household with five kids, it is to be expected that the *whole* truth does not come easily.

My fifteen-year-old son and his twelve-year-old brother are typical boys: always pushing each other's buttons. The younger of the two is pretty quick to up the ante physically while the older one tends to be more subtle. So one day when my teenager tripped his younger brother and then rather loudly called him a "klutz," the twelve-year-old responded with a powerful and painful punch. My older son no doubt knew his younger brother would take it too far and be the one to get in more trouble, but when I tried to get the whole story, I was not immediately successful. While the older one was willing to admit the "klutz" remark, no doubt because it was loud enough for me to hear, he did not admit to having tripped his brother in the first place. You have to work at the whole truth in a household with lots of kids.

I have to add, too, that no one in my house ever admits to eating the last cookie (sometimes me), finishing the ice cream, or using the last of the toilet paper without replacing the roll.

The whole truth rarely comes easily. We tell our children they must admit to the entire story, though, because we all know that the blue fairy was right when she told Pinocchio, "A lie keeps growing until it's as plain as the nose on your face." Call it damage control, but confessing the entire story is always the best course of action. For our nation's leaders, this is a difficult endeavor. It is not always easy to determine when the story ends. The audience is constantly changing. The truth also is colored by interpretation, the conviction of one's beliefs, and party politics. Leaders believe that they act for a greater good. Sometimes telling the entire truth is not prudent, depending on the circumstances.

Yet, Americans crave transparency in their government. Americans rationalize that if a leader is not afraid of admitting the truth, chances are you can trust him. Is that not the essence of why we tell our children to tell the truth, so we can trust them? Americans are jaded by the recent past and less trustful of their government these days. We question what we were told about the reasons we went to war in Iraq. We question what we have been told about the terrorist threat from al-Qa'ida and how well we are doing against it. We question whether our government's actions since 9/11 have made us safer or have instead made more enemies.

The problem is that the truth we seek is not very satisfying. Understanding the reality of the world we live in does not make our choices any easier. When our children are leading America, perhaps the best we can hope for is that they will be humble enough to admit that the truth is unclear. At least if they communicate the uncertainties, Americans would be more likely to trust them. That would make them great public servants even if they never win a political party's endorsement.

Party politics is tricky when it comes to telling the whole truth. The solutions to most foreign policy and national security challenges do not fall neatly into a single party line. The need for politicians to explain their way as the best way is often what causes them to obscure the whole truth. If they tell us that part of their party's course of action could have negative consequences, we are going to be less likely to endorse them. Better to skip that part of the discussion. The baby wipe cleans far more things in my house than it was ever intended to, but it sure does not do the laundry. A single set of policy options cannot magically clean up the world.

Our national security and foreign policy initiatives since 9/11 have been dominated by a "war on terror." Whether you agree with the terminology or not, the point has been to focus most of our energies on countering terrorism and very few people would argue with the rationale for that. As one of a small group inside the Intelligence Community warning fifteen years ago about the terrorist trends, I certainly would not argue with the need for significantly enhanced counterterrorism efforts. But I also would not paint them as obvious options. Our children learn something very basic in elementary school science: every action causes an equal and opposite reaction. That physical reality can be applied to foreign policies as well. Whether intended or not, whether avoidable or not, the reactions to our actions are real and should not be ignored.

The initial focus of the "war on terror" was on al-Qa'ida, its leadership in Afghanistan, and the Taliban regime that harbored them. The aggressive actions of the United States and our allies significantly disrupted and damaged the group's capabilities, infrastructure, leadership, cadre, training, planning, and communications. This could have been a turning point in discrediting the extremist ideology al-Qa'ida stood for and in demythologizing bin Laden. But the destruction of al-Qa'ida was not complete.

It is helpful to understand that terrorist groups are small groups of tightly knit people. Often they are made up of family members and childhood friends. Members trust each other implicitly and easily spot an outsider. Terrorists rely on each other for survival. They know to protect their identities, their communications, their homes, families, and friends. They live very secret lives because their lives literally depend upon secrecy. Al-Qa'ida is one such organization. Destroying al-Qa'ida was never going to be an easy task. Most terrorist groups are never completely destroyed by the governments working against them. Their ideologies over time become stale and bankrupt, and they erode from within. What was always going to make the complete destruction of al-Qa'ida difficult was the dispersal of its key members in so many locations around the world. Even a crushing defeat in Afghanistan would have left a lot of work still to be done.

Regardless, the defeat in Afghanistan was only partial. The US intervention in Iraq diverted significant US resources from what had been a focused effort against al-Qa'ida. At the same time, the images of US forces in Iraq were quickly exploited by al-Qa'ida and others to promote the idea that the United States was really at war with Muslims, not terrorists. That sentiment was a huge boost to al-Qa'ida and its extreme, anti-US ideology. The US was painted as an occupying force, not a liberation force, in the heart of the Muslim Arab world. Bin Laden himself could not have been more convincing than many of the images produced in Iraq. Other aspects of the "war on terror," particularly the incidents that took place at Abu Ghurayb, questions surrounding the detention facility in Guantanamo, arrests and renditions of suspects across national boundaries, and secret detention centers, along with the public disclosure of wiretapping in the United States, all fueled the theory that the US was at war with Muslims.

Raising these points is not intended to criticize the decision to go to war in Iraq in the first place. The issue is telling the whole truth. We ask our children to reveal the whole story even though parts of it may undercut their position. In the example I pointed out earlier, I know my older son was reluctant to admit he tripped his brother because he knew it would undercut his argument that when his brother punched him hard, it was disproportionate to his crime of calling him a klutz. But the truth was that my older son started the physical attack when he stuck out his foot to trip his brother. Regarding the war with Iraq, Americans might have agreed that the benefits of removing Saddam Hussein were worth the costs if the entire list of risks and benefits were transparently conveyed to them, including the potential for a setback in our defeat of al-Qa'ida in Afghanistan and Pakistan and an increase in hostility toward the United States. But the point is, we will never know because the discussion was too limited.

We face an evolving threat that will continue to challenge us and force us to make difficult national security decisions. For one thing, al-Qa'ida is still with us. And now we also have to face individuals who have either been to Iraq or are anti-US because they believe the United States is at war with Muslims. Finally, there are isolated groups and networks of individuals who believe they can give more weight to their local extremist agendas by joining forces with globally known groups like al-Qa'ida. Some of these developments have been the unintended consequences of our "war on terror." That's part of the whole truth.

When we teach our children to admit to the truth, we are teaching them that only complete honesty can bring lasting peace of mind. Only honesty earns us respect. If they apply these principles when they are in charge of America, maybe they will demonstrate that honesty, which comes from humility, also can bring lasting peace in the world.

Chapter Eight

If you make the mess, clean it up

When our children are our nation's leaders, they will know that US actions in the world are not always neat and clean. We make messes, not all of them intentional. But when we do, who should we expect to clean them up but ourselves?

Chapter Eight

If you make the mess, clean it up

I HAVE A FRIEND WITH A SIGN THAT STATES, "A CLEAN house is a sign of a wasted life." I get it. Striving for that perfect concept of "everything has a place and everything in its place" is a stretch in a house with five kids and a dog. It also would require spending a lot of hours a week just cleaning. I'm not able, nor am I really willing, to spend that much time cleaning when I have so many other more important demands on my time. One thing I do strive for, though, is getting my kids to clean up after themselves. My three-year-old can sing the Barney clean-up song and put her toys away, but it seems the older my kids get, the less enthusiastic they are about cleaning up their messes. I wish Hannah Montana and the Jonas Brothers sang clean-up songs, maybe that would motivate them. Until then, it is always the same struggle. I just want them to be responsible for the mess they made. I don't ask anyone to wash my coffee mug or do my laundry. No one ever has to clean up the sewing area after I've made Halloween costumes. I never demand that my kids make my bed or put my clothes away. Despite setting a good example of cleaning up after myself, my kids have yet to learn this lesson.

When I had to go on my first work-related trip after my first son was born, I cried. I couldn't stand the thought of leaving him behind for a week and being in a foreign country and unable to talk to him all day long. By the time my third child was born, I had to suppress my glee when called away for work travel. After all, staying in a quiet, clean hotel room while taking a bath with a glass of wine and leaving the television off is as good as a day at the spa. I also secretly enjoy the thought that my children (and my husband) are being forced to clean up after themselves. No mom to do a dozen loads of laundry, throw away the piles of junk mail and newspapers, or put the Legos away so they don't get vacuumed. I console myself with the idea that at least for a week, they are realizing how much time I spend keeping the house in order. If only they would remember that when I get back!

Let's assume some children do learn to be responsible for their actions, even when those actions create a mess. When they are our nation's leaders, they will know that the United State's actions in the world are not always neat and clean. We make messes, not all of them intentional. But when we do, who should we expect to clean them up but ourselves?

Iraq has created a vortex of impossible foreign policy choices for the US. The situation is tenuous and unclear. The country may remain on the brink of civil war for years, with a significant incident igniting a downward spiral at any time. Some argue that the only thing preventing Iraq from devolving into a full-scale civil war is the US military presence. If this is true, then Iraq is more likely to undergo a civil war if US forces leave suddenly. We may be able to blame the fighting on the parties involved rather than ourselves.

It is also possible that a slow and fragile political process will emerge in Iraq over a long period of time. With each passing year, a little more stability is achieved though a lot of turmoil and violence would still be evident. A significant presence by the US military as a stabilizing force and deterrent to a civil war likely would be part of this picture. A possible model to compare to Iraq would be Algeria in the 1990s. Algeria experienced over a decade of civil war and significant bloodshed involving terrorism even while the central government continued to function.

The challenges for Iraqis are daunting. They need to engender public buy-in to the political process and trust in national politics even at the expense of sectarian goals. They need to moderate their expectations, create a rule of law that satisfies all parties, and restore day-to-day basic services and security across the country. Elections—the skeleton of a democracy—are not enough. To thrive it must have flesh and blood.

The challenges Iraq poses to the US are equally as daunting. We need to succeed in Iraq. But we need to leave as well to both satisfy public expectations and wishes and to prevent Iraq from continuing to be a magnet for terrorists and an incubator of anti-US hostility. Any form of success in Iraq likely will be a failure on other levels, particularly if you try to measure progress over short periods of time. Is success merely bringing the troops home? Is it ensuring Iraq, or parts of it, don't become another terrorist safe haven like Taliban-controlled Afghanistan was? Is it leaving behind a security apparatus in Baghdad dedicated to upholding the rule of law and committed to preventing ethnic cleansing? Is it leaving a central government that is functioning and running all parts of Iraq? Is it exiting Iraq and not watching civil war begin as we move out?

Rather than thinking about Iraq in terms of successes, another way is to examine which types of failure we can tolerate. If we don't defeat the terrorists there, are we willing to risk that they will regroup and attack us here? If we leave Iraq and it devolves into civil war or another authoritarian regime comes to power, can we live with a failed democracy?

If I suspend reality for a moment and trust that my children will learn to clean up after themselves, then I can imagine how they might handle Iraq. Each of my kids is unique and they would define "clean" in different ways. My older daughter, for example, is very literal. A clean room is a precise thing. When forced to clean her room, she starts from scratch, quite literally pulling everything off her shelves and everything out of her closet. She sorts and purges, reorganizes and decorates along the way. It takes a long time and no one can even open the door to her room during the process. But it is a beautiful thing to behold when she's done. I have no doubt she would stay in Iraq no matter what the costs until she left the country an ideal nation and a model of democracy. The messes she would create along the way, like the bags of things she leaves outside her room for me to throw away, would still have to be dealt with. Iraq would be perfect, but it is hard to say how much of the rest of the world she would have messed up in the process or how much of the US economy would be bankrupted to pay for the cleaning.

My second son is the polar opposite. Clean, like beauty, is in the eye of the beholder. If everything fits under the bed and he can find all his clothes, toys, and school stuff when he wants them, then the room is clean. In fact, to him that is perfection, especially if I don't look under the bed. I can imagine the Iraq he would leave behind. Underneath a veneer of stability, his quick departure would leave behind issues still needing to be resolved and messes just ready to eke out. He would be satisfied, though, because the rest could always be cleaned on another day and a lot of US taxpayer money would have been saved in the process.

In the next year, America will have to choose which kind of clean it is willing to live with in Iraq. There are sacrifices and risks to either course.

CHAPTER NINE

Don't give in to a bully

The world did not fundamentally change on 9/11. America did not witness over two hundred years of strength eroded by one terrorist attack.

CHAPTER NINE

Don't give in to a bully

EVERY SUMMER YOU CAN GUARANTEE THERE WILL BE AT least one blockbuster film that will feature a bully. The theme has been around in literature since David and Goliath. I would like to do the research to see if there are differences in the way male and female authors approach the topic. I think even moms would have to admit there is a certain satisfaction from watching the poor kid who has been bullied and beaten throughout the movie finally clobbering his tormenter in the end, a la *Karate Kid* or *A Christmas Story*.

My favorite bully stories tend to end a little differently, though. I like *Ever After*, which ends with the Cinderella character telling her stepmother, who is about to be condemned to a life of servitude, "I want you to know that after this moment, I will never think of you again." What complete victory for Cinderella to rob her evil stepmother of any influence in her life whatsoever.

My twelve-year-old son took a different tack in disarming a "bully" when he was in kindergarten. My son sat every day on the bus with his friend who lived next door. Nothing unusual in that, but they were faced with a boy who got on the bus at a later stop who picked on them. When my son brought this to my attention, at first I was alarmed. He had just turned five! To have to deal with a bully so young in life! But then I realized that the boy who was teasing him had been a friend in preschool. I explained to my son that most likely the boy was just feeling left out because they had been friends. He was probably a bit jealous that my son was already sitting with another friend every day. My son's solution to the problem was to invite the other boy to play after school and get re-acquainted. It worked out great and they remain friends.

Envy is often at the root of bullying. Someone who perceives himself as weak is jealous of someone he believes is strong. Someone who believes himself to be unpopular envies someone who is generally well-liked. While the kid bullied in most movies is typically depicted as physically weak, they are most often the morally grounded one and the character who is the better role model. The weak bully the strong to make themselves feel stronger.

Terrorists are inherently weak. Their ideology of violence and hatred is usually unpopular. They typically lack conventional military strength or the infrastructure support that comes with government status. They use terrorism as a substitute for real strength. They use the media coverage as a replacement for popular credibility and legitimacy. Terrorists feed off of the reactions of their victims, the media, and the world that is watching. They derive "strength" from the focus they receive. By saying al-Qa'ida is a grave threat to our national security we elevate their capabilities, as if they are strong enough to threaten the greatest military power in the world. That is how they drive us—by sowing fear. But the world did not fundamentally change on 9/11. America did not witness over two hundred years of strength eroded by one terrorist attack.

America need not be afraid. We know there are risks in being a strong, engaged democratic world power. There are two ways to defeat terrorism. We can disengage from the world and by giving up our role as a leader of nations, we become insignificant. Terrorists will not be attracted to attacking us if we are perceived as weak. They only need attack the strong. Our other option is to not be afraid.

When we tell our children not to give in to a bully, we teach them to be true to themselves and think for themselves. They need to understand that the lesson can be painful and hard. The bully may take a swing or say something that really hurts for a long time. But we teach our children that if they give in to the bully, they are giving up on themselves and their beliefs. If the bully is wrong, giving in only serves to legitimize his taunts. Our soldiers, diplomats, and intelligence professionals do their best to protect us from "bullies" of all kinds, but American citizens have to be willing to do their part: to not be afraid.

Chapter Ten

Choose your friends wisely

We can disagree with our friends and remain friends. What we cannot do is control how others will perceive the relationship.

CHAPTER TEN

Choose your friends wisely

MY DAUGHTER'S FOURTH-GRADE TEACHER RECENTLY CALLED me with distressing news about my daughter's behavior at school. She described my daughter, as other teachers have characterized her, as a follower. Unfortunately, she followed the actions and words of a group of girls who landed in hot water with their teacher. They had said things that were disrespectful and rude. I'm still sorting through the best course of action to take with my daughter, but I know what the goal is. Her teacher said as much—"She needs to learn to think for herself."

My daughter's friends are smart and usually sweet little girls. They make mistakes like everyone, and how they chose to interact with their teacher on one odd occasion is not really a fair depiction of who they are. But the incident is an opportunity for me to teach my daughter two very important things. You must choose your friends wisely because they shape the person you are going to become, and you must think for yourself regardless of how much you love and respect the people around you. When my daughter grows up, I hope she will demonstrate that she has learned these lessons. If she is ever president of the United States, I hope she leads our nation choosing our allies wisely and ensuring America thinks for itself regardless of how important and close those relationships are.

In the "war on terror," America has chosen its friends based on a number of factors. We have looked at historical allies who have been through trials and tribulations with us and proven loyal. We have looked at nations who have been threatened like us and have formed friendships based on mutual interest and have chosen to become closer friends than we might otherwise be. Each of these friendships benefits America. But each also comes with strings.

As with friendships, we often accept that by choosing friends, we choose our enemies too. An enemy of my friend is my enemy also. In world affairs, being tied to the agendas and enemies of our allies does not always serve our larger interests. We can disagree with our friends and remain friends. What we cannot do is control how others will perceive the relationship. When our friends pursue a course that we disagree with, it is difficult to convince the rest of the world that we are not supportive. Similarly, when our allies cling to policies that fundamentally contradict our own democratic principles, it is challenging to explain to an observing world how we can justify the continued friendship.

For example, India is the most populous democracy in the world and a close ally of the United States. Yet India has refused since 1948 to hold a plebiscite demanded by the United Nations to determine the fate of Kashmiris, many of whom want their own state rather than be ruled by India. Pakistan, another US ally, has aggravated the Kashmir situation over the years by supporting Kashmiris engaged in guerrilla warfare against India. Both nations want Kashmir to be part of their state. Kashmiris themselves are split on the issue. But the United States believes in the self-determination of people. Only the mandate of the people should determine the future state of Kashmir.

For years, American policies in the Middle East have rung hollow to the populations there. We say we support freedom of speech, a free press, self-determination of people, a fair judiciary, and the right to vote. Yet we support regimes year after year that intentionally block those rights. We take the side of the regimes because we believe it is in the best interest of America. We can and probably will continue to do so because these regimes are our allies. They have helped us when we needed it and many of their agendas coincide with our own. But just as I want my daughter to remain friends with girls who are intelligent, nicely behaved, and caring, I also want her to be able to think for herself. I want her to choose her own course of action and use her own voice.

When America stands by its allies, it should feel confident that it can use its own voice, too. Our friends disagree with us in public. We can take a different stand and say so. The United States on occasion disagrees with the United Kingdom and even Canada, but we are able to do so without harming our relations. We should be able to differ from our other allies without fearing we will lose a friend. If these governments break relations with us because we criticize some of their actions, then they were not really the friends we thought they were.

CHAPTER ELEVEN

If you can't say something nice, don't say anything at all

A president can no longer have two different conversations, one with the American public and one with the rest of the world. It is a real challenge to rattle your enemy and speak the truth about uncertainties to your constituency at the same time.

Chapter Eleven

If you can't say something nice, don't say anything at all

I WAS THE YOUNGEST OF FIVE AND HAD THREE OLDER brothers. I never could understand why my brothers bothered talking to me at all. It felt that their vocabulary was limited to teasing words. Why say anything to me when it would have been less energy not to talk? Sadly, I see this same trend playing out with my own kids. And as with my experience, it tends to be the boys who find endless pleasure in tormenting their ten-year-old sister. I realize the key is because girls care what is said about them, and we could end this cycle by just ignoring our obnoxious brothers. I tell my daughter this every time, but to no avail. She still cries or stamps her foot, and storms off mad and hurt.

The funny thing about the command, "if you can't say something nice, don't say anything at all," is that it actually appeals to a child's natural tendency to be lazy. Why bother wasting your breath if it's only going to get you into trouble? I cannot understand why they do not follow this rule. Like any other mom, when one of my kids says something unkind to the other, I remind them of how they would feel if someone said that to them, especially if the person saying it was someone they cared about and respected. This is one of those lessons, though, like telling them to wear their coats in winter, which is best learned through tough love. Tough love can work in one of two ways. The first is that the offender ends up being insulted by someone else in a similar way. Then they do feel the pain they previously inflicted. With any luck, they remember it and hold their tongue the next time they're tempted to say something mean. The other way tough love occurs in my family is that the insult comes back around in a different way. If my twelve-year-old son tells my ten-year-old daughter that her new computer game is "stupid," just watch how quickly she refuses to share it when some other time he decides it looks like fun. How easily we become victims of our own rhetoric.

Rhetoric spoken by a world leader can be extremely powerful in either a positive or negative direction. Think of Khrushchev's statement in 1956: "Whether you like it or not, history is on our side, and we will bury you." Taken as an extraordinarily belligerent statement, ironically Khrushchev claimed he meant something different: that communism would outlast capitalism. In the end, the subtleties and context did not matter. That statement galvanized America. As my teenager would say, America responded with a resounding, "Not." But there are other times when a leader's statement can box a nation into a course of action that it soon discovers is not in its best interest. Many have argued that the war terminology currently used to describe our counterterrorism efforts have had negative consequences.

For our leaders to give a speech in today's world of global communications is more challenging than even a generation ago. A president can no longer have two different conversations, one with the American public and one with the rest of the world. It is a real challenge to rattle your enemy and speak the truth about uncertainties to your constituency at the same time. It is difficult in a time when the American people demand an immediate response by their government. Yet, the words of world leaders at critical moments can be powerful because they influence future events. They almost always require careful crafting, just as a parent reminds his child in a critical situation, "think before you speak."

In contrast, there are times when words can carry very little meaning. Sometimes separating the noise from something worth listening to is the real challenge. I have to prevent myself from being overly critical with my kids because occasionally I fall into a pattern of only offering corrections to my children (and husband) and forgetting how important it is for them to receive my praise. But in a big and busy family, it can feel like there is only time to communicate essentials. Yet my kids quickly start tuning out everything I say when all they hear is criticism.

My mom always told me not to criticize. Most of the time she said that in reaction to my critiquing her, but I know she was also trying to teach me that if I criticize others, I better be prepared for them to criticize me. But criticism, though painful at times, can also be a catalyst for reflection and self-improvement. Criticism of America, likewise, can prompt debate and reflection that eventually leads people to a richer understanding of America's principles and policy positions.

Often, criticism is most easily found in the media. America has long championed a free press as a foundation for promoting free speech and encouraging debate of ideas. More voices are better than one. Just as my kids tune me out when all they hear is "noise," the more noise, the less likely people are to hear the extremist fringe. The more voices, the more likely people are to find the one that represents their concerns. Extremists cannot monopolize the ideas of the people when there is a thriving free press.

The expression of ideas that are not our own should not threaten our beliefs. We can choose not to listen. So why does the al-Jazirah news network seem to irritate us so? The more outlets created in parts of the world that have suffered from autocratic governments, the more likely it becomes that the central voice of the populations are going to be heard. The people in the region need an opportunity to voice their views and be informed free of the control of their governments. A broader range of ideas will surface. The people would be able to voice their views, debate their merits, and find their "center." Extremists—whether in governments or in the opposition—would drown in a sea of free speech and unrestricted flow of ideas.

CHAPTER TWELVE

Learn from your mistakes

Ultimately, the real mistake we may have made in the aftermath of 9/11 was to allow the terrorists to shake our faith in ourselves. If we have learned from this one mistake, then we must know now that as long as we hold true to our democratic principles and have faith in each other, America will be secure no matter what challenges we face.

CHAPTER TWELVE

Learn from your mistakes

MY FATHER TAUGHT ME TO LEARN FROM MY MISTAKES WHEN I was in fifth grade in a way I would never forget. I had an assignment in my social studies class to write a one-page essay on a research topic. I went to my dad and asked him the question. He gave me a fairly elaborate response, but I was able to follow most of it and recount his tale in my essay, which I turned into my teacher the next day. I failed. My dad, who was a real proponent of "tough love," purposely gave me the wrong answer. In tears, I asked him why. "Because it was your homework assignment, not mine," he said. I should have done the research myself.

Trust me, I never made that mistake again. In fact, for quite a while, I did not ask my dad a thing.

The attacks on 9/11 were an extraordinary event. It is to be expected that a nation reacting to such an attack would make choices. Action was required. But our national security should not be defined in narrow terms as the absence of terrorist attacks. Defining our national security as the commitment to our national identity would ensure our security endures. Including a commitment to national prosperity—as part of that identity—projects the real strength of America, embodied in our democratic principles and core values. The welfare of a nation's economy and populace plays a significant role in its security. No nation would be considered truly secure if its government was bankrupt and its citizens lived in poverty and need. All that we do as Americans to boost our economy and care for our neighbors is a contribution to our nation's security, and every American is part of our national security apparatus when we recognize that our security flows from the health of the country.

Linking our national security to the prosperity of our nation and its people allows every American to contribute to securing our nation; our security flows from the health of the country. There are many nationwide initiatives that involve us all. One example would be elevating the urgency with which America eliminates its dependence on foreign oil. Just as America led the world during the Industrial Revolution and in revolutionizing the communications and computer technology industries, we could be the leaders in the energy revolution. Securing independent energy sources for centuries to come would not only free America from dependence on oil-producing countries but also imagine making nuclear power unnecessary, undermining the ability of rogue nations to exploit energy needs for development of weapons.

Another way in which our welfare and security are linked is through the efforts of the federal government to ensure the continuity of its services to its citizens. By "leading a unified national effort to ensure the continuity of federal government services to Americans in the event of a disaster or attack," we are "preserving our freedom, protecting America…and securing our homeland." The quotes are derived from the mission statement of the Department of Homeland Security. The organizations that make up the Department have always provided essential citizen services—one way in which the government strives to guarantee the health and welfare of the American people.

Perhaps the most important way we can strengthen our national security is by civic participation. Our state and local governments and private sector have tremendous capacity to project America's influence abroad. Our world has become a much more close-knit place. There are over twenty foreign consulates in Atlanta, Georgia, for example. American cities wield increasing economic and political influence in other nations and all instruments of American power extend to a mayor's office.

Direct involvement of state and local governments with foreign communities facing similar risks and challenges would project influence in new ways. Tailored assistance and exchange programs between such communities could have more influence than generic and overly ambitious national ones. The Virginia Corps, for example, recognizes that the federal government cannot do it all and offers a model of local mobilization and responsible citizenry for small countries or communities abroad. New York launched ReliefWeb even before 9/11 to provide an online gateway for information on humanitarian emergencies and disasters. ReliefWeb harnesses the experience of New Yorkers in facing disaster to aid communities in crisis around the world. One can imagine a direct dialogue between local leaders in New Orleans and Islamabad, who share similar experiences in handling overwhelming natural disasters.

Ultimately, the real mistake we may have made in the aftermath of 9/11 was to allow the terrorists to shake our faith in ourselves. Our national security is guaranteed by the strength of America's character, integrity, and trust in democracy. If we have learned from this one mistake, then we must know now that as long as we hold true to our democratic principles and have faith in each other, America will be secure no matter what challenges we face.

When we tell our children to learn from their mistakes, we are teaching them how to obtain wisdom. America is still a very young nation. Much like a teenager anxious to make its presence felt, America sometimes acts with good intentions but with limited time spent thinking through all the potential ramifications of its course of action. Making mistakes is also part of maturing as a nation. But learning from those mistakes is essential if we are to remain a leader of nations.

PART THREE

The Strength of a Nation Derives from the Integrity of the Home[4]

4 Confucius

NATIONAL SECURITY MOM
MOM

Part Three

The Strength of a Nation Derives from the Integrity of the Home

Over 2,500 years ago the Chinese philosopher Confucius said it all. His quote is as true today as it was in his time. But in today's debates about our nation's security, we rarely discuss the role of an individual family. So the question is: how can we translate these words of wisdom into action?

Having explored how the principles of parenting apply to national security and how the advice we give our children can make our nation stronger, this final section underscores the need for American families to participate in their governance. While most of the discussion looks at how parents in general have important expertise to contribute to government, it focuses in particular on encouraging women and mothers because statistics highlight the persistent gap in the number of women in politics. This is not intended to downplay the important contribution of fathers or the tremendous progress our generation alone has made in narrowing the gap between the involvement of men and women in parenting.

CHAPTER THIRTEEN

Bows from which living arrows are sent forth[5]

5 With apologies to Khalil Gibran whose phrase was really, "You are the bows from which your children as living arrows are sent forth."

If being willing to approach national security from a different point of view is "soft," then I am as proud to be soft as I am of my twenty years working the "harder side" in intelligence. Balancing the two is critical. I believe that to resolve problems, we have to understand them first.

CHAPTER THIRTEEN

Bows from which living arrows are sent forth

THIS QUOTE FROM THE POET KHALIL GIBRAN IS SIMILAR TO a line from Psalm 127 that also describes children as the arrows and parents as bows. Both sayings are powerful reminders of how fleeting our time is with our children. They also remind us that our kids are not things we own, but from the moment we bring them home from the hospital, they struggle to be independent of us.

Golda Meir added her twist to the theme when she said, "Women's liberation is just a lot of foolishness. It's men who are discriminated against. They can't bear children.

And no one is likely to do anything about that." How true. I know at each of my children's deliveries, there was a moment when I thanked God that I was a woman and could do what no man could ever do. Of course, there were moments when I cursed that fact as well. But, overall, I would never trade places with my husband. To give birth is to experience the closest thing there is to being the Creator. For a brief moment when you hear your baby's voice for the first time, you realize what you have done, and you feel omnipotent.

Juxtapose that thought with the scene from the tear-jerker *Steel Magnolias*, when Sally Field's character says after her daughter is removed from her life-support system and passes away, "I find it amusing. Men are supposed to be made out of steel or something. I just sat there…there was no noise, no tremble, just peace. Oh God. I realize as a woman how lucky I am. I was there when that wonderful creature drifted into my life and I was there when she drifted out."

Yes, it's only a movie, but it captures one of the essential differences in the way men and women show their strength. A woman demonstrates her strength most powerfully when she surrenders to her child. A woman submits to her child during pregnancy and does whatever it takes to birth a healthy baby. She spends her entire life putting that child's needs before her own—a lifetime of servitude. A mother watches her beloved child get hurt, experience heartbreak and disappointment over and over again. And if tragedy strikes and the child dies, the mom will have to accept that her baby was never really hers to begin with. Instead, it was a privilege and a blessing to have been given the opportunity to be a mother. Yet, submission is not typically considered a sign of strength.

My cousin lost her only child, who was pregnant at the time, in a tragic accident. I've never seen such a tower of strength when I watched her gently touch the casket of her only child as if to thank her for the little time they had together. Since that day, she's never given into grief. She's lived each day with love and shows extraordinary patience toward everyone. When I think of the trivial nature of so many of my complaints, I blush with embarrassment. She never complains, though she has so much to complain about. That is strength.

My sister-in-law gave birth to twin girls prematurely. She held her daughters in her arms for the few hours they lived, accepting that whatever time she had with them was a blessing. That is the strength of a mother.

In all my years in the Intelligence Community, I have seen many displays of courage. But one woman's example still sends me to work every day. For a brief period in the early 1990s, I was involved in analyzing the terrorist activities of Libya. In 1991, Libya was indicted for its role in the 1988 Pan Am Flight 103 bombing, but Libya was also well-known for conducting harassment and even assassination campaigns against Libyan political dissidents. So when a Libyan dissident and leader of a human rights group, Mansur Kikhia, was reported missing in December 1993 from his hotel room in Egypt, his family, friends, and colleagues feared the worst. Weeks after Mr. Kikhia disappeared, his wife, an American citizen, approached government officials for help in discovering what happened to her husband. I was one of the people she met.

Mrs. Kikhia is an incredibly brave woman. I have never known anyone else like her. She went to Egypt and retraced her husband's steps, determined to find out what had happened to him, and she didn't care if it cost her own life. She boldly visited Libya and Egypt several times in her quest to determine her husband's fate. And although she probably knew in her heart that her husband was dead, she never gave up her search for the truth. The State Department concluded in "Patterns of Global Terrorism" that Mr. Kikhia was believed to have been executed by the Libyan regime. Mrs. Kikhia's unwavering commitment to uncovering the whole truth, no matter how painful or dangerous, inspired me. She is one of the reasons I go to work every day. Her example of strength and perseverance motivates me to do all I can to prevent having to watch another woman suffer what she has.

Women are unbelievably strong. I do not mind that my husband can lift more than me and open jars that I can't. It doesn't intimidate me that he can drive the car faster and better or that he knows how to handle a gun and I don't. I am not embarrassed that I hate mice and snakes or that I almost always feel sick when the kids have thrown up. My strength is different than my husband's. Not better, just different.

It is a simple fact that mothers cannot be fathers because women cannot be men. But often you will hear a woman talk "tough" on an issue that is generally considered the purview of a man simply because the world expects "tough talk." It is very common in national security, foreign policy, and counterterrorism to hear women try to "out-tough-talk" men to avoid being considered "soft." Anything other than belligerent speech is considered soft, which is automatically perceived to be weak. But as the previous chapters point out, strength and security come from more than just physical might.

If being willing to approach national security from a different point of view is "soft," then I am as proud to be soft as I am of my twenty years working the "harder side" in intelligence. Balancing the two is critical. I believe that to resolve problems, we have to understand them first. I prefer to accept that American policies have had bad results in some places rather than sticking my head in the sand. I do not believe a war of attrition can defeat terrorism. I believe it demonstrates more character to allow people whose beliefs you reject have their say; it takes more integrity to admit you've made mistakes; and it takes far more courage to refuse to change in the face of a threat. I am a mother and that is the strength I know. That is the definition of strength that I will pass on to my children so that they understand there is a balance.

Chapter Fourteen

A man's work is from sun to sun, but a mother's work is never done

---

We refuse to be enablers of the myth that parenting comes more easily to a woman so men should not be expected to do it as well. Men and women bring different approaches—the combination is powerful.

CHAPTER FOURTEEN

A man's work is from sun to sun, but a mother's work is never done

I WAS WORKING IN THE INTELLIGENCE COMMUNITY WHEN my first son was born in 1993. My husband, who was a public relations specialist at the time, was working for a small, nonprofit trade association. He had just left a big public relations agency for something more personal and rewarding and was very happy with his move. Neither of us were prepared for being parents and we certainly had no way of knowing all the decisions we would have to make in that first year: Day care or nanny? Full-time or part-time? HMO or PPO? Move closer to work or find a house with a yard?

When my eight weeks of sick leave came to an end, I was physically and emotionally unprepared to go back to work full-time. My husband and I scaled back every expense we could so that I could work half days for another four weeks, and he convinced his new office to let him work half days from home. At eight weeks old, our son became a baton we handed off mid-day in Washington, DC, where we both worked. The poor child rode the metro back and forth from our home just so my husband and I could maximize our time in the office.

During that period, we found a new day care center opening up around the corner from my husband's DC office. If it had not been new, we never would have been able to find day care for our son so quickly. In this area, most parents reserve space before they even get pregnant. Nonetheless, we got lucky. The facility was nice enough and the care providers were all very capable and kind, but we hated it. And our son seemed to hate it, too. He had never exhibited signs of separation anxiety beforehand, but within a week, he started crying furiously whenever I left his sight. My husband and I were both miserable.

After surviving four weeks of day care, I remember the morning I was packing my son's bag, fighting back the tears when the phone rang. My mother, who was attending the funeral of a cousin in New York, had just gone to the hospital after suffering a heart attack. Within a couple of hours, my husband, son, and I were packed and in the car on the way to New York.

I stayed with my dad and siblings for a few weeks while my mother recovered. I think seeing her grandson every day was a real comfort to her. I'm glad we were there. But going home and back to the day care and the separation anxiety was much harder after being away from it. After a few weeks of being with my son again all day, I could not bear to give him up to total strangers who would get to share the vast majority of his waking hours.

So my husband and I had the same conversation so many first-time parents have over whether we could afford to be a one-income family. We knew we wanted to have more children, so it seemed logical that I would be the stay-at-home mom. There would then be no career to disrupt with subsequent maternity leaves. But I had the stable federal government job, with good health care and job security. I also had a job that could not be done from home because of the classified nature of the work. My husband, on the other hand, could switch to private public relations consulting and work out of the house.

Fortunately for us, when my husband approached his boss with the fact that he would be quitting work to stay at home and raise his son, his boss—a forward thinker for the time—suggested he just do his current job from his house instead. So my husband became a pioneer in the telecommuting trend that had only begun to hit America. Although my husband had a babysitter from time-to-time to help a few hours a week at the house, he was the primary caregiver. He was also the primary breadwinner since his job paid more than mine. He was lucky to have more flexibility in terms of hours and where he could work. My son was lucky because my husband is really the more patient disciplinarian. Everyone won.

It was during this period in the mid-to-late 1990s that my husband observed that women are often their own worst enemies. While my husband was raising our son and managing a successful career, his job very often had him interacting with women at both work and home. Female colleagues around the country were amazed that he was doing his job from home while caring for his son. When he arranged playdates and took our son to the park, he never ran into another stay-at-home dad, but plenty of moms. Always he found that the women, whether mothers or not, were amazed that he was doing what he was doing. They lavishly praised his open-mindedness, calling him a "Renaissance dad." He liked all this at first and felt genuinely appreciative. But he eventually became insulted by the repeated implication that men were not inherently capable of being primary caregivers for their children. He bristled at the idea that men all over America were universally perceived by their wives as shirking on their parental responsibilities. And in the end, he blamed these women for enabling the very thing they complained so bitterly about. If they think it's so amazing for a man to be a stay-at-home dad, then that's what men will think. Women were sending the message that being a fully engaged dad is too hard and only a few men are cut out to do it.

My husband argued that women should spend less time praising him and start expecting their husbands to do more of the parenting—and without thanking them for it. He remarked that it's not as if men go around thanking their wives every time they change the kid's diaper, and he couldn't understand why women feel so compelled to praise their husbands when they participate in the mundane aspects of parenthood. My husband did not disagree when I offered that women tend to "mother" their husbands. We do not like to admit it, but we encourage them to do what we want them to do by using the old mothering trick of positive reinforcement. It's not as if we can take away their allowance or put them in time-out (although I will admit, I have employed the "time-out" from the obvious inducement when I got really desperate).

However, I have seen changes in this trend in the past fifteen years. Many of the dads in our little neighborhood are as engaged in parenting as the moms. Certainly even the fathers with the traditional day job away from the house are more involved in the mundane duties of household chores, chauffeuring kids from one sporting event to another, and playing non-stop peek-a-boo. I hope this is true in other neighborhoods across America. As my husband suggested in 1993, now we do not praise or even bother to thank our husbands for changing a diaper that's so wet that it's doubles the child's overall weight. We refuse to be enablers of the myth that parenting comes more easily to a woman so men should not be expected to do it as well. After all these years, I think we have learned that men and women bring different approaches to parenting and that the combination is what can be so powerful.

The author of the quote, "A man's work is from sun to sun, but a mother's work is never done" is unknown. Perhaps someday the concept that parenting is mainly the mother's job will become so old-fashioned that the quote will be obsolete.

Chapter Fifteen

The hand that rocks the cradle is the hand that rules the world[6]

6 W.R. Wallace

Our public servants need our guidance, not only because they answer to us, but because they need the help. And who can be better than parents when it comes to helping those in office now build a better future for our kids?

Chapter Fifteen

The hand that rocks the cradle is the hand that rules the world

It's time to move onto challenging another myth and to bring new life to W.R. Wallace's quote. According to the Center for American Women and Politics at Rutgers University, in 2008 women hold only 16.3% of the seats in Congress; 16% of the Senate seats; 23.5% of the statewide elective executive offices across the country; 23.7% of the state legislative positions; and of the mayors of the hundred largest cities in America, only eleven are women. A woman has never been Secretary of Defense, Treasury, Veteran Affairs, or Homeland Security. A woman has never been vice president or president of the United

States. Clearly, women are not equally engaged in the governing of their community, their state, or their nation. We can blame history, the educational system, men, and many other legitimate underlying factors for why this is the case. But we also have to ask ourselves whether our disengagement perpetuates the myth that men are somehow more naturally suited to govern.

It can seem intimidating to be politically involved, even at the local level. On the one hand, there's so little time for yet another activity. Keeping up with the issues is time-consuming for busy moms answering to the real needs of their kids. On the other hand, government seems to be dominated by the views of people who do nothing but engage in government and politics. The "talking heads" you hear on television, radio, and whose views you read in newspapers and magazines are not stay-at-home moms or working mothers struggling to get home in time to take their daughters to ballet class. The statistics from Rutgers tell the story: most of the people engaged in American politics and government are men.

The funny thing is that running a nation, a state, a city, or a small town is not that much different than running a household. In fact, towns, cities, states, and even our nation, are just different combinations of households. From a purely logical perspective, mothers are probably better prepared than anyone to be presidents, governors, congressional representatives, and mayors. For some reason, we tend to not translate our experience and expertise in managing a home into governing our community and nation. But rather, we allow ourselves to be intimidated by the political jargon and the military-influenced concept of security, believing we don't know enough to voice our opinions.

To govern means literally, "to rule by right of authority; to exercise a directing or restraining influence over; guide." Sound familiar? I have the authority in my house to rule. I exercise direction and certainly have a restraining influence on the behavior of my kids. I do my best to guide. When I think about it, I have been governing a mini-state of seven constituents, not to mention the many guest residents in my mini-state of "Bennettland." Fortunately, I have a partner. My husband is sometimes my vice president, sometimes my chief law enforcement officer. He is almost always the transportation secretary and on occasion, he is a budget advisor. But even he would admit that I am the one who sets the direction. A president is "an officer appointed or elected to preside over an organized body of persons." My family is not exactly an "organized body of persons," but for the sake of the argument, I do preside, that is, exercise management control over them.

One thing I have learned from presiding over the Bennett household is that you have to prioritize horizontally. Multi-tasking is an essential skill. It sounds pretty basic, but with eight baseball games a week, another nine practices, seven dance classes, a music class, and weekly Sunday school, not to mention homework, PTA, and the countless other volunteer activities, the day can get away from me. So yes, my husband and I have been known on occasion to ask at nine o'clock at night, did we feed everybody today? And on at least one occasion, our six-year-old son has told us in the morning that we forgot to feed him dinner the night before.

Multi-tasking is not optional if you are a parent. In a large family, you have to be really good at it. I cannot very well miss my six-year-old's first baseball game just because I have to accompany my high-school student's Model UN orientation. I find a way to do both (and no, the Intelligence Community has not figured out how to clone mothers). I have to thank my kids for making me an expert at multi-tasking. It has been an essential skill at work as a terrorism analyst. I have found myself guiding fellow officers in Afghanistan, Iraq, and far beyond while simultaneously digesting an endless mound of reports from various intelligence sources, and drafting analysis for national security policymakers to read the next day. This is accomplished often while mentoring junior colleagues through the process and trying to answer the call from the school nurse about the "little incident" that took place on the playground.

Parents are the world's most capable multi-taskers. We may resent the word and hate the concept, but we know we do it because everything really is a priority right now. And each of our kids is equally important. If you look at any type of executive job in the government, from town council chairperson to the mayor of a big city, you'd find the job description sounds a lot like what a parent does. From budgeting to local planned development, moms and mayors have a lot in common, such as trying to figure out how to make the checkbook cover both your son's college savings fund and the orthodontic device your daughter needs now to prevent erosion of her teeth later. When the unplanned occurs or the income isn't what was expected for the month, you have to make cuts and tighten belts. It's a guarantee your local mayor is facing the same issues. Those prioritization and organizational skills you hone as a parent are exactly what any executive officer in government desperately needs to succeed.

From the town council to the state legislature, our government leaders are trying to do it all because their constituents expect them to. As voters, we want our government representatives to be responsive to our needs. We want them to fix our roads, but we also want them to enlarge the cafeteria at the forty-year-old elementary school so our kids do not have to eat lunch at 10:00 in the morning. We want Congress to appropriate funding for education and health care, but we also want to reduce the debt left to our kids.

Parents can govern because they already do it every day. We just have to believe that governing our community, our city, our state, and our nation are an extension of how we govern our household. We have to see that we have the skill set, expertise, and judgment, and not let jargon be the obstacle. If you can decipher your toddler's speech and sing, "head, shoulders, knees, and toes" you can learn the alphabet soup of government acronyms. If you can figure out how to save ten dollars a week by buying your family's favorite cereal on sale in large quantities and purchasing all the paper products somewhere other than the grocery store, "obligating funds" until the "windfall money" comes at the end of the "fiscal year" would be a breeze in comparison. And if the idea of a press conference, with aggressive reporters throwing hard questions in your face every few seconds seems intimidating, just consider the two hours in the car you spent trapped with your three-year-old who never stopped demanding that you respond to her endless string of completely unrelated questions with the answers she wanted to hear.

We may not all be ready to run for mayor or Congress, but being engaged in our own governance is not just about taking on public office. Our public servants need our guidance, not only because they answer to us, but because they need the help. And who can be better than moms when it comes to helping those in office now build a bright future for our kids? All politics are local and national security is no exception. When we make a decision at the community level, like lobbying for more money for schools, we are sending a message about what we believe is important to our nation. Signing the PTA petition to persuade the town council to not cut the elementary school budget *is* engaging in the debate over national security.

In addition to governing, a parent also has extensive experience in conflict resolution. Even mothers of single children have to navigate conflict with their kids' friends. I'm lucky—with five kids, I have plenty of opportunities to hone my conflict resolution skills at home. My two older boys do not fight often. They are both engaged in such different activities that they are not even around each other that much. But when they do fight, it can quickly reach a serious intensity. The older one loves to provoke, and the younger one can't control his temper. Unfortunately for my older son, his younger brother is not smaller. He is quite muscular and can do some serious damage when he has rage on his side.

When I hear it get out of hand, I may have to send in the tanks (my husband) to stop the fighting at first, but I usually follow in the conflict resolution role. I facilitate the negotiations by forcing the boys to sit down and take turns with their version of the story, not allowing the other to interrupt. Just the time it takes to go through these elaborately staged versions does the trick of calming them down physically. As a shrewd negotiator, I pride myself on keeping track of the logical flaws in their stories and picking those apart. It does not take long for the stories to change and we eventually get to the bottom of the issue. As with conflicts between nations, perceived property ownership is often at the bottom of the battles between my boys.

When the United States deliberates over whether to send in troops or ask the United Nations to intervene, the conflicts are complicated. But at the heart of it is usually the same issues mothers deal with every day. Perceptions of discrimination, violation of property, unfair treatment, provocative behavior of a long-standing antagonist, and limited access to fundamental needs, like water, are frequently the root cause of conflict between nations. Negotiators are doing the same thing a parent does during a time-out: trying to assess the situation objectively and offer suggestions for a permanent solution between the warring parties.

Next time you pick up the paper and see a headline about a flare-up between Sunni and Shia neighborhoods in Iraq or between factions in Darfur, try reading it from a parent's point of view. Think of the parties involved as your children, each with very different but legitimate grievances. How would you resolve the situation? What would you say or do to convince the parties that you can be fair in listening to both sides? What would you say to the parents of each faction, knowing that they are doing everything they can to improve the lives of their children who are trying to survive the worst of circumstances? An advanced degree in international relations is not a prerequisite for compassion.

CHAPTER SIXTEEN

We must be the change we wish to see[7]

7 Mohandas Karamchand (Mahatma) Gandhi

We know the secret to

keeping the world going is

never surrendering to

"I can't do it" or "I hate you."

Moms hope when everyone

else has given up.

Chapter Sixteen

We must be the change we wish to see

DURING A VISIT TO MOROCCO, I WAS WANDERING AROUND in the crowded streets of the old walled city of Fez. It was amazing to people-watch in a city so far from home. I happened to pass a small pastry shop just as a young mother was exiting. In one hand she was balancing a large, heavy-looking tray of pastries. In the other hand, she held tightly to the hand of a little boy who must have been about three. He was crying and dragging his body and digging in his heels, making it very difficult for his poor mother. I had to smile as I watched them struggle in front of me and I'll admit I slowed down so I could observe how she handled her little boy's tantrum. Fortunately for her, they didn't have far to go and I saw her turn left toward a door that was flung open. It must have been her home because I saw what appeared to be her husband standing just inside the doorway. His face bore the unmistakable irritation you would see on any dad in such a situation. I would not have been surprised if he'd said, "Now what does he want?"

I have always believed that people are basically the same the world over, and watching that family in Fez brought it home for me so vividly. I have done exactly what that woman did: ignored the tantrum and just kept on going, longing to be home as quickly as possible and hoping no one would take any notice of my screaming appendage. I've seen that exasperated look on my husband's face over and over as he hoped against all odds that the noise would stop.

All around the world, parents persevere. We make it through countless temper tantrums and scraped knees. We sing the same theme song to the latest television show with enthusiasm ten thousand times. We say, "don't whine," a million times a year. We wash the same clothes over and over and make the same macaroni and cheese dinner. Above all, we never tire of giving hugs.

There are always attempts to bring our world together. We've had dialogues on every imaginable issue: a "dialogue of religions," "dialogue of nations," "dialogue on hunger and poverty." All of these are noble goals.

I would like to add one more: a dialogue of moms. Instead of having a world conference to solve a problem, we could have a worldwide exchange of our experiences as mothers. We could share our thoughts without trying to win an argument or sign a treaty. Observers and foreign policy experts might scratch their heads and ask, "What was the point of that?" but we would walk away more informed, connected, and enlightened. Since mothers don't put a lot of faith in the quick fix, we would value the investment in enhancing mutual understanding.

Moms are engaged for the long haul. We know our influence is critical to the next generation of Americans and leaders across the world—and the generation after that. Our tenacity and our faith in our children make us stronger than any army. We teach our children to be good citizens and we prepare them to be our nation's leaders. We know the secret to keeping the world going is never surrendering to "I can't do it" or "I hate you." Moms hope when everyone else has given up.

The fact that moms hope when others give up may be why we see so many charitable organizations led by mothers and women determined to help other women and their children. As moms, we watch our babies pull themselves up to their feet and proudly take their first steps. In those first few days and weeks, we nervously watch for falls and are always ready to scoop them up to the safety of our arms. And then the months and years pass and we watch them drive off in our car. Then their world, and ours, is changed forever. Moms know it only takes "baby steps" to change the world. Each and every charitable organization, every dollar or hour we donate to a worthy cause changes the world. As long as we persist and continue to have faith that we can do it, the falls along the way will long be forgotten.

So every time we ring in a new year, start school, or enter a new administration in America, parents hope for a better world. When these important passages of time occur, I try to take a few minutes to admire my kids. For a brief moment, I can suspend all the realities of temper tantrums, sibling rivalries, academic challenges, and other worries and see all the wonderful possibilities their futures hold. I never give up hoping that they might be able to solve the problems that today we think are intractable.

I believe our nation's security will be in good hands with our children someday because I believe in today's moms. If we define our national security as something that flows from the strength of America's character and integrity as a nation, then no army or intelligence organization can do what we do to secure our nation. As the first and most influential teachers of the next generation of America's citizenry and leaders, we will determine the course of our future.

There will be difficult lessons. When we tell our children to ignore the schoolyard bully, we know in our hearts they might still get hurt in their quest for self-respect. We can't teach them that being strong is easy. Just as the playground will always have bullies, the world will always have dangerous people who use threats and force to get attention. The source of their effectiveness comes from their ability to produce fear. There will always be people like bin Laden, twisting and distorting religions and ideologies to serve their personal ambitions. These terrorists do not fear death or destruction and all the intelligence and military power in the world will not wipe them out. No amount of money or resources is enough to create a perfect system for detecting terrorist threats. Terrorists strike in every kind of country, from the most repressive prison states to the most democratic.

Nonetheless, terrorists do fear one thing. They fear being irrelevant. They only have influence if someone is paying attention to them. They only have power if they can make people afraid. The only way to truly defeat a terrorist, therefore, is to ignore him. Oddly enough, that is the one thing within our power as individuals and as a nation to do. But it takes a lot of courage and commitment to strike back in this way. And a lot of hope.

Each and every day we spend *without* thinking about terrorism, the terrorists lose. Every time we make a choice about traveling, for example, without being afraid, the terrorists lose. Every time a mom in America tells her child that courage is standing up to a bully and ignoring him, the terrorists lose. As long as we persevere, the moms of America will render bin Laden and all terrorists like him irrelevant. And that will be their ultimate defeat.

ACKNOWLEDGEMENTS

I have so many people to thank, but I have to start with my dear friend and fellow "fairy godmother," Sue Malone, for improving my first draft and inspiring me with her unique blend of humility and strength. Also thanks to Sean and Maggie for their contributions! A huge thanks to Nancy Cleary who helped me overcome my biggest fear—that of being in the public. And to Erika Kotite whose encouragement led me to Nancy and Wyatt-MacKenzie Publishing where I found a network of incredibly resourceful and supportive women.

Many thanks to Vince Lupo and Kim Reyes for their support and making me smile! And to Cynthia Donavin, the moms, instuctors, and dancers at her Classical Ballet Academy for showing me how truly beautiful strength can be.

I would also like to thank Suzanne Spaulding and Hyon Kim for their support and insight; and Barbara Sude, the entire Kohn family, and all my dear friends in the neighborhood and CTC for believing in the idea that parenting and national security really did have something in common!

There are many others at work and home—my sister and sisters-in-law, nieces, cousins, aunts, and mother-in-law, and my entire family and many colleagues—whose seemingly quiet lives inspired me. I have tried to capture their strength and wisdom and their dedication to parenthood and national security. But it would be impossible to do them justice so I hope they forgive my brief attempt. I also am so grateful to Ruhi Ramazani who taught me how to analyze from the day I walked into his classroom at the University of Virginia, and to his wife Nesta, whose life of commitment to Thomas Jefferson's principles inspires so many.

To my husband and kids, I owe my greatest thanks. They are my story. And they gave up so much "mommy" time so I could write it. I know not even a big vacation will make up for all the times I said, "not now" (but start planning your dream vacation, kids, because I owe you!).

I have to thank my father, though he is no longer with me, for teaching me the meaning of service to my country. Never complaining, never wavering, he taught me that we commit to the greater good for the sake of the greater good, never for personal gain or acknowledgement. And to my mom, who believed in me as only a mother can whenever I stopped believing in myself. What better example of motherhood could there be?

INDEX

Everything We Need To Know About NATIONAL SECURITY We Can Learn From Our Kids!

Tell the Truth

When kids tell the truth, they remind us that telling all sides of every story is the way to be a well-respected world leader.

Choose Your Friends Wisely

Kids act like the crowd they hang with... so do world leaders.

Actions Speak Louder than Words

Kids know that what we do matters more than what we say...an important lesson in leadership.

Clean Up Your Own Mess

As kids take responsibilite for themselves and the places they go, they show us how to make the world a better place for all.

Don't Give In To A Bully

If kids have the courage to ignore the schoolyard bully, then perhaps we can all rob the terrorists of their power by refusing to give in to fear.

You Could Be President Someday!

When kids participate in their school elections, they inspire us to be good citizens by using the ultimate power of our voice, especially through our vote!

illustrated by
KELLEY CUNNINGHAM

from the book written by
GINA M. BENNETT

www.NationalSecurityMom.com

Wyatt-MacKenzie Publishing

Printed in the United States
134464LV00001B/92/P

9 781932 279726